For Nicola

CONTENTS

'A tree that it takes both arms to encircle grew from a tiny rootlet. A pagoda of nine storeys was erected by placing small bricks. A journey of three thousand miles begins with one step.'

Lao Tzu, from the *Tao Te Ching*

Your Best Career Starts Here

When you think about how much time we spend at work each week, it seems strange that we put so little of it into thinking about our career. It may be because careers can seem like curious creatures. When we leave school or college it's inconceivable that one day we'll be retiring, and when we're in the thick of things it's just as hard to look more than one step ahead. I don't know about you, but when I'm experiencing the middle of winter I struggle to remember what last summer felt like. Did I really walk around in shorts and a t-shirt, and not feel the cold?

But just as inevitably as the seasons come around, there will arrive a day when you look back on your working life and evaluate it. How will you feel? What will you think? Regrets you may have a few, but I hope not too many. Your aim should be to feel proud of what you've accomplished over the previous sixty-odd years. To achieve this takes energy, positivity and just a little courage – qualities I'll be exploring throughout this book.

While I was researching it I came across an interesting story about David Bowie. Some documentary film-makers had discovered that he'd auditioned for the BBC back in 1965. In those days, anyone wanting to perform had to be approved by the corporation's Talent Selection Group, a committee of – shall we say – somewhat crusty, traditional men who were responsible for ensuring that any act appearing on the radio was of an acceptable standard.

What was their verdict? 'A singer devoid of personality,' wrote one. 'Singer not particularly exciting. Routines dull,' noted another. Sadly, poor Bowie (then still called Davy Jones) failed the test, but he didn't let this hold him back. Four years later, he was to find global fame with his 1969 album *David Bowie* and the single 'Space Oddity'. The rest, as we know, is music history.

It would be fair to say that David Bowie is a shining example of someone who took charge of his career and of his destiny. He had a famously reinventive approach to his work, and in one of the archive clips that was uncovered he's quoted as saying, 'I spent all my formative years adopting guises and changing roles, just learning to be somebody.' It is now more than fifty years since he released that first album and, as a reporter in *The Times* noted, his 'early stumbles show that bad reviews are merely a temporary setback'. He also kept working until the very end, with his final album *Blackstar* being released just days before his death in 2016.

You too can paint the canvas of your career just like Bowie did – it really is within your ability. But to do this you need to know things that you didn't learn at school or university, which is why I've written this book. As the Chairman of REED Recruitment, I've helped millions of people find work, and in doing so have built a billion-pound business. I've also worked in the jobs market for over twenty-five years now – that's a quarter of a century of immersion in other people's careers. Through the thousands of conversations I've had with job-seekers, recruiters, workers and business leaders, I've been lucky enough to pick up some valuable wisdom that you won't find collected anywhere but here. There are so many successful people out there with equally brilliant career journeys. Why not learn from them? Their careers have been the result of hundreds of small decisions made along the way. Decisions that have made them into the people they are today.

You may be starting out in your working life and wondering what your first step should be. You may also be asking yourself when 'working' becomes a career. Or you could be mid-journey, enjoying the fruits of your experience but not sure whether you want to continue in the same direction. Perhaps you're a few years from retirement and your heart is set on one last transition (or even to wind down in a way that feels right for you). Whatever your situation, I aim to bring you a mixture of challenge and motivation, helping you to feel confident and then to do something powerful with your self-belief. This is how you will fulfil your potential and make a success both of your work and the rest of your life.

WHAT KIND OF CAREER SEEKER ARE YOU?

At this point, let's take a short and good-natured diversion on the road to career success by working out if we can spot the different types of career seekers who roam the corridors of pretty much every organisation. Can you spot any familiar figures? And which one are you?

The bewildered student

Characteristics: emerges blinking from the sheltered confines of school or university, only to gulp at the thought of facing the 'real world'.

Strengths: a blank sheet of paper, ready and willing to write their dream career upon it. They're up for anything as long as it brings in a bit of money and provides experience and excitement.

Weaknesses: they haven't a clue what they want to do, and don't have any experience in doing it either.

Next steps: throw yourself into whatever opportunities you can to learn, travel and develop. It's more about what you learn than what you earn at this stage.

Missing in action

Characteristics: having achieved the dream of being promoted through several roles and gaining valuable experience, this careerist has discovered that what they wanted when they first started is now losing its shine. Pastures new are on the agenda, but which ones and how to find them?

Strengths: they know what they're good at and have confidence that they have something special to offer an organisation.

Weaknesses: they're just not sure what that something is, and it's eating away at them.

Next steps: take a breath and congratulate yourself on what you've achieved so far. Then examine your passions, values and purpose in life. What career could both match those and give you the fulfilment that's escaping you right now?

The ostrich

Characteristics: obsessed with their work, this person has their nose to the grindstone 24/7. They think nothing of answering emails over dinner, working weekends as well as all week, and burying themselves in the minutiae of their industry.

Strengths: hugely experienced, and valuable to any organisation that cherishes commitment and hard work over anything else.

Weaknesses: by sticking their head in the ground and never glancing up to see what's over the horizon, this worker runs the risk of being taken by surprise by changes in their company or sector. Just as worryingly, they'll be missing all sorts of opportunities that are staring them in the face.

Next steps: stop, look up and glance around. Meet people – any people. Ask questions and listen to them. You'll be amazed at what you learn.

The easy lifer

Characteristics: never happier than when chatting by the water cooler or scrolling down their newsfeed on work time, this clock-watcher has the secret dream of marrying a rich celebrity and living the life to which they believe they're entitled.

Strengths: none that are obvious, although their hours spent finding ways to avoid work have given them skills in persuasiveness and networking that would rival a salesperson extraordinaire.

Weaknesses: with a lazy attitude to their career, they're unlikely to go far. And that's a shame, because their false preconceptions of work as being boring and unfulfilling will therefore be confirmed.

Next steps: if you're happy like this, then fine. But if not, consider what more you could give to your organisation and try it. You never know, you might find it gives you something valuable in return.

The fired fifty-something

Characteristics: having settled comfortably into the assumption that the next twenty years would hold more of the same, this career mid-lifer has a rude awakening when the scythe of redundancy sweeps their organisation.

Strengths: tons of experience, which can be applied to a variety of roles and workplaces.

Weaknesses: the opposite of the proverbial boy scout, this person is completely unprepared.

Next steps: it's going to be OK. Your achievements will follow you wherever you go – you just need to gather your wits and plan your next steps. The path to retirement doesn't always run smooth.

Do you recognise yourself, even just a little bit, in there? Or maybe you're a combination of two or three of these people. Whatever your discovery, it's good to be straight with yourself because that's where the learning begins.

BE A HAVE-A-GO HERO

I've developed much of my approach to life by learning from my father, Alec Reed, whom you'll see popping up occasionally throughout this book. Alec has always been prepared to give things a go. As well as founding REED and various other business ventures, he also set up a charity website called The Big Give. How it came about is certainly an example of the saying, 'nothing ventured, nothing gained'. Wanting to do something more for charity, he invited a group of philanthropists to a two-hour brainstorming session, promising to buy them lunch in return. They spent a couple of hours exploring ideas for new charities, but when the time was up there was no firm conclusion. Just as they were standing up to go to lunch, one of them said to him, 'You should set up a virtual charity.'

My father mulled over this comment as they walked to the restaurant and realised that he didn't have the faintest idea what the man had meant. 'What do you mean, a virtual charity?' he asked as they sat down to eat. 'Oh, I haven't a clue,' replied his guest. My father chuckled at this, but the suggestion triggered an idea to create an online platform that charities could use to showcase their appeals. The hope was that donors with deep pockets would window-shop for the ones they wanted to support, without having to contact the charities directly and feel under pressure to donate. The Big Give was born.

At first it was pretty uneventful – the website gained one donation of £100,000, which made everyone excited, but that was it. Then my father had another idea, which was that he'd give a million pounds from his own charitable foundation to match whatever the other charities were able to raise through the site. He knew he was onto something when his money was matched within just forty-five minutes of opening the appeal, and that's how The Big Give took off. Today it's the leading match funding platform and has raised over £100 million for thousands of different charities. Our ambition is for it to have raised over a billion pounds one day.

The lesson from this is that it's always important to give something a go if you feel strongly about it. Never assume that it's not possible, because even if it doesn't work out you'll learn and grow from the experience. People who take charge of their careers are what I like to call 'have-a-go heroes', and if you don't feel terribly heroic right now you may find yourself becoming more so by the end of this book. I hope so, and can guarantee that you'll be more than capable of surprising yourself.

THE FIVE FUNDAMENTALS OF
CAREER SUCCESS

If you think of your career as being a road trip, 'having a go' is the fuel that drives your car and the Five Fundamentals are the rules of the road that you need to know to reach your destination. So, what are these rules?

1. **Be ambitious**

   The word 'ambitious' sometimes has a bad press, but I don't see it as being negative or grasping. To me it means having high expectations of yourself and of the place you work. Where do you see yourself in the future? What do you plan to give and receive throughout your life and career? One of the currencies you can trade in is ideas, which make up the most precious resource any organisation can have. The more ideas you have and the better you implement them, the more ambitious you can afford to be.

2. **Be a powerhouse of positivity**

   There's plenty of scientific evidence to show that positive thinking affects every aspect of your life, and especially your career. The more meaningful you believe your work to be, the better you'll feel both mentally and physically – it's a virtuous circle. This is allied to having a growth mindset, in which you stay open to learning and developing throughout your life.

   You've never had as many opportunities to improve and learn as you do now, because the world of self-education – one of the keys to a successful career – is available to you at all times. There are blogs, books and videos on a multitude of topics at your fingertips. Use them to teach yourself about whatever you want to focus on, and if you struggle with feeling demotivated, read about that as well!

Not only do you have the opportunity to learn, you can also achieve more than you think you're capable of. On most days we don't even reach 40 per cent of our capacity, both physical and mental, but I'm sure you've experienced moments when you reached a new level just because you had to rise to a challenge. There's an inner courage within each one of us and we surely have to connect with it. I call it being spirited. This is the spark that ignites the fire that will propel you forward.

3.   Understand yourself and your organisation

Whether you're aware of it or not, you have enormous strengths within you, ranging from what you know (being good at maths or art, for instance) to the qualities you have (integrity, curiosity and determination). Understanding yourself means that you have an insight into what you can offer a job or organisation. Where could you make yourself most useful, and in what way? Knowing where your strengths lie opens up opportunities for you, because you'll start to see what a wide range of roles you can claim as your own.

There's no use, however, in being clear on what you have to offer if you're not equally knowledgeable about the place you plan to work. When you apply for a job, you're thinking of committing a considerable amount of your time and energy to that organisation. At a party recently, I was chatting to a woman who asked me how a particular company was doing, and she was amazed when I took out my phone and looked up their accounts online. Anyone can do this, and if you're wanting to enter into a long-term relationship with a company (for that's what it is), you should do your due diligence.

4. Know your supports

Try this for an interesting question. In your career, who's helping you move forward and who's holding you back? Your answers will prompt a re-evaluation of who you hang around with and whose company you actively seek out.

There is so much support around us, but we don't always see it. Close friends and family are obvious, but there are bound to be other people who you've met in different contexts and who you might have forgotten. Think about the clubs you've joined, the activities you've taken part in, the jobs you've done, and the places you've studied. All contain potential sources of help and advice.

5. Lead yourself

You may or may not aspire to be a leader of others in the future, but one person you must learn to lead is yourself. That means organising yourself, being proactive, not settling for second best, and discovering what you need to do to have the career that you want. Another way of looking at this is to be self-reliant, self-motivated, self-disciplined and self-aware.

Does this all seem a bit, well, self-centred? Yes,

possibly. But who else is going to make sure that you wake up each working day looking forward to the hours ahead? It's down to you to make it happen and this book will help you along the way.

MY AMBITION FOR YOU

Now it's my turn to be ambitious, because my sincere hope for you is that you'll leave *Life's Work* with insights that will help you to power ahead in your own career. I want you to think, 'I can do this', or 'I see how that works now, I'll give it a try'. If you feel moved to change the way you approach your career in a positive way, you will spot opportunities more easily than you did before. That's success in action.

You'll see that each of the twelve chapters is based on a command (you can think of them as the Twelve Career Commandments if you like). And at the end of each chapter are five bullet points that summarise the key messages, totalling sixty easily accessible, golden career nuggets. If you use them wisely they'll help you to enrich your career for the better and to change your life for good.

You'll also find a couple of questions relating to what you've just read, called 'And just asking'. These will help you to apply what you've learned to your own career and life, so you can start putting your new knowledge into practice straightaway.

CHAPTER 1

Look in the Mirror

Working in the recruitment business, I talk to people about their careers almost daily. It's rare that I come across someone who says that they knew exactly what they wanted to do when they left school, and is on the same trajectory decades later. Life isn't like that, and it would probably be boring if it was. As one of the top professors at Harvard Business School, Lynda Applegate, once said to me, 'Straight roads aren't as interesting as winding ones.'

The people I do meet frequently are those who started off on the wrong career footing for one simple reason: they didn't think about what would fulfil them in their work. This led them to make the wrong decisions, such as taking a job their parents wanted them to do, or a role that was well paid but that they didn't enjoy. I don't want you to make the same mistake, which is why we're starting off with a process of self-reflection. A little self-knowledge and awareness will take you a long way, so carrying out a personal audit is an excellent place to begin. After all, when you decide upon your life's work you first need to know what fires you up.

This applies wherever you are in life. A friend's son came to see me recently because he was at a crossroads in his career and was unsure what to do next. I could see his confidence was at a low ebb, as is often the case in these circumstances. If you've been in his shoes you'll know what I mean. You might have lost your job, felt disappointed that your previous role wasn't what you expected, or maybe your organisation changed in a way that didn't suit you. I suggested to this young man that he was at a 'look in the mirror' moment, and that doing what I'm about to describe to you might help him decide on his next steps.

I'd suggest that, unlike this man, you don't leave looking in the mirror until you're forced into it, because it's much easier to carry out a self-evaluation when you're in a positive frame of mind. And you can do it as often as you like – most of the elements are relevant whatever your age or stage. When you're thinking about what you want to do with your time on earth, there's no rule that says you can only do this introspection in your twenties.

I appreciate that you might want to run from the idea of carrying out a self-analysis. Most people do. Apart from anything else it sounds self-obsessed, doesn't it? I understand, but the word 'self' has an undeservedly bad press in my opinion. What I'm talking about here is self-focused leadership; not in a 'look at me, aren't I amazing' way, but in a constructively self-critical way. This is the best form of criticism, because when you do it to yourself it's a lot more palatable than when someone else does it for you. Whenever I talk about this in front of groups and ask people, 'Who likes to be criticised?' no one ever raises their hand. But when you open yourself up to some gentle evaluation by *you*, it can be different. The theme of self-criticism runs through this book, so it's a good idea to grow used to it from the beginning.

In fact there are many words you'll come across through-out the following chapters, all of them beginning with 'self'. Self-motivation, self-analysis, self-confidence, self-criticism, self-determination, self-development, self-esteem, self-improvement, self-mastery, self-reliance, self-focused leadership – the list goes on. There's nothing wrong with 'self' in these contexts, because by focusing inwards you're learning the skills to lead and inspire others as well as advancing your own career.

MIRROR, MIRROR ON THE WALL . . .

Let's take a look at what this 'look in the mirror' thing is all about. I'm going to lead you through a four-step process for gaining an understanding of who you are. I know that you might be tempted to skip this because it sounds strange and involves a deliberate effort to do something practical. But all this means is that, if you're one of the few who do go through it, you'll have an edge over all the other people who don't. At the least you'll begin to have an understanding of yourself that will stand you in good stead for the future, and at the most you'll find it life-changing. With this kind of upside, I'd say that it's worth half an hour of your time.

Step 1: find a mirror

You're going to carry out this exercise looking in an actual mirror. Please find one and take a long look at yourself for ten minutes – this is who you are, literally. In a world in which attention spans are increasingly short this may feel like a tough exercise, but the more you look the more you'll see. This isn't about judging the size of your nose or working out if you're attractive enough, although those thoughts may cross your mind. It's about seeing beyond that into your soul and appreciating who you really are. When you've done this write down what came to mind.

Many years ago I did this exercise as part of a group mindfulness session, in which we had to study ourselves in detail. I gazed at the lines on my face, my eyes, and everything about my appearance. Although I started off feeling as if it was almost impossible to do, I relaxed into it and found that I was appreciating myself more and more because I realised that, just like you, I have something special. I'm the only one of me there is, which makes me unique. You're the only one of 'you' there is, which makes you unique. Distinctiveness is of great value.

Step 2: identify your passions

Now you'll start to work out what you love and hate in life, both in terms of what you do and who you do it with. This is important, because your emotions and enthusiasms create the energy that will drive your future success. To help you I've created a list of questions. Your answers to these questions will give you new ideas and inspiration. You can also ask others close to you to offer suggestions – it's always helpful to gain extra input.

- What are you good at? *You can think about what people tell you you're good at, as well as what you think yourself.*
- What fascinates you? *Think about the topics and ideas you feel compelled to spend time investigating.*
- What do you put off doing? *What tasks and chores do you dread?*
- What annoys you when you see it done badly? *It's obvious to you, but perhaps not to everyone else.*
- If you were given a day to do whatever you wanted, what would it be?
- Which kinds of people do you enjoy spending time with?

The most important thing is to be honest with yourself. If your ideal day consists of baking cakes and chatting with friends, that's fine; don't feel you have to come up with something that might sound worthy for the sake of it. No one will see these answers apart from you, and if the responses are genuine they'll be starting to give you clues about what to do with your remaining time, which is the rest of your life.

Now you're going to come up with a list of five things you love to do and five you hate, using the insights you've gained from the exercise above (and anything else that comes to mind). They can be anything in your family, social and work life. For instance, you might love country walks, reading books, filing paperwork, cooking and researching holidays, and you might hate crowded shops, loud music, working for overbearing bosses, people who talk too much, and fiddling with numbers. List them here in a few words.

Your loves

1. _____

2. _____

3. _____

4. _____

5. _____

Your hates

1. _____

2. _____

3. _____

4. _____

5. _____

You're starting to build a picture of what makes you tick. Have you unearthed anything you wouldn't have expected?

Step 3: work out your values

Values are like invisible but indestructible threads, pulling us in specific directions but without us knowing. It's important to lift the veil on our values because if we're not conscious of what those threads are, we may find ourselves taking wrong turns in life. There's nothing worse than ending up in a job that conflicts with your values because it gives you an uneasy feeling from the word go. There's that nagging sensation that something's not right, and it can lead to internal conflict.

Given that values are invisible, how do we identify them? Luckily they have a habit of revealing themselves in what we choose to do and how we think. Try answering these questions to uncover yours.

• What's the main reason that you work, apart from the money?

- If you were king or queen for a day and could change one thing in the world, what would it be?
- What three qualities would you love everyone to benefit from? *For instance, good health, fulfilment and freedom.*

Hopefully this has sparked some thoughts about what's especially important to you, and the helpful thing is that our values rarely change as the years go by because they often have their roots in our childhood. The way we express them might fluctuate, but their nature is pretty constant. To round off this step, use the insights you've gained from the earlier exercises to list your top three values. Bear in mind that there are many you could consider to be important, but only a small number you would feel personally committed to putting into practice. As an example, when I did this exercise I realised that mine were honesty, kindness, and persistence.

1. _____

2. _____

3. _____

Step 4: pinpoint your purpose

Your passions and values all come together to form your overarching purpose. This isn't just for your career; it's for your whole life, so it's worth spending some time reflecting on what it could be. For instance, if you've identified that you love sports and socialising, and feel that continuous self-improvement is one of your key values, your purpose might be 'bringing people together through sport' or 'harnessing sport for positive social change'. Or if you have a passion for books, hate loud people, and are committed to the idea of equality for all, your purpose might be 'everyone deserves the opportunity to enjoy reading'.

At this point you may be wondering if this is all a bit pie in the sky. 'Come on,' you may be thinking. 'We can't all spend our careers saving lives and creating world peace. Be practical.' I understand that. Sometimes you'll be in a position in which you have to go after a job because it's what you need right now, whether it serves your higher purpose or not. But you should always be looking to move your career in the direction you feel most strongly about. If you can't find some fulfilment in the ultimate purpose of what you do, you won't commit to it heart and soul. And when you're not fully dedicated, you won't do as well at it. We can all tell the difference between a person who's just treading water and someone who's up for swimming the English Channel because they're driven to succeed.

It's for this reason that most successful organisations have a clearly defined purpose. IKEA's is 'to create a better everyday life for the many people', BUPA's is 'longer, healthier, happier lives', and Nike's is 'to bring inspiration and innovation to every athlete in the world. If you have a body, you are an athlete.' I don't know about you, but I feel uplifted just reading those.

How about more examples, this time from successful individuals? Sir Richard Branson says his purpose is 'to have fun in my journey through life and to learn from my mistakes'. Oprah Winfrey's is 'to be a teacher, and to be known for inspiring my students to be more than they thought they could be'. These people have achieved more than many of us will do in a lifetime, and how they've done it is to be clear on what they're about. You can also see how their passions and values shine through, with Branson's emphasis on fun and acceptance, and Oprah's on teaching and encouragement. Inspiring stuff.

I was once asked, 'What's your family's purpose?' I have to admit that at the time this stumped me. 'Good question, I'll get back to you on that one,' was my reply. But it got me thinking, and we discussed it as a family. We agreed that we felt strongly about wanting to build businesses that would be of benefit to society, and that we enjoyed connecting people to each other for good. You can see how this works well for an entrepreneurial family, and having this clarity about what we do is helpful when it comes to making business and career decisions. When you're at a crossroads, or any decision point, you can ask yourself, 'Is this option supportive of my overarching purpose?' Many alternatives will drop away, which makes your path so much more clear.

Write down your purpose here.

'My purpose is _____

_____

_____

_____ ,

WHAT NEXT?

I'd encourage you to spend quite a bit of time on this process before you turn the page. After you've done so, it's possible you might have come to the conclusion that the career you've set your heart on isn't the right one for you. Or it may have left you feeling unsure of what road to take now that you've developed new insights about yourself. This can be unsettling, but it's better to know this now than in five years' time when you're feeling inexplicably miserable in your job. Your passions, values and purpose are your compass points in life, guiding you to the best decisions at the appropriate times, so your career choices must dovetail with them.

When you look in the mirror you're saying, 'Who am I? Who do I want to be? And how am I going to become that person?' These are big questions and you won't know all the answers yet, but you've made a start. Learning what you're 'about' is a deep and open-ended exploration that you can engage in at any age or stage of life, and I suggest you revisit it on a regular basis.

Once, when watching *Match of the Day*, I was inspired by ex-footballer Alan Shearer who said that the Manchester United players needed to take a long, hard look in the mirror every morning and ask themselves the following question: 'How am I going to give my best today?' And in the evening they should do the same, but with a different question: 'Did I deliver for the team?' It's worth noting that in the weeks following the match they changed coach and then went on to win an unprecedented eight games in a row. You may not be a million-pound striker, but you can still tap into your own spirit and your own life force by using this power of reflection.

WHAT WE COVERED

- Self-reflection is the vital first step in planning your career, because it's only through self-knowledge that you'll be able to make the right decisions.
- First, look in a physical mirror and learn to appreciate yourself.
- Second, identify your loves and hates, which provide the power source for your progress.
- Third, work out your values, which give you fulfilment in your work.
- Fourth, pinpoint your purpose, which will steer you in the right direction.

AND JUST ASKING . . .

- What's the most surprising thing you've learned about yourself through doing this exercise?
- What changes might you make to your plans, now that you know more about yourself?

CHAPTER 2

Go to Parties

'Go on, it'll be fun,' he said.

'I don't think so, you go without me,' I replied. 'I'll just stay in and watch the football.'

'Come on, everyone's going to be there. And it's just a couple of drinks. It'll do you good to get out.'

'No really, I'll be fine.'

'You'll regret it.'

A pause.

'Hmmm, OK,' I replied. 'Just for an hour. Then I'm off home, OK?'

'Great!'

'Give me a minute to get changed and we'll go.'

The day was a cold, grey, winter Wednesday a long time ago. I'd just come home from work, and my cousin Tom was in the process of persuading me to go out for drinks with him and a few friends. You're probably wondering why I'm telling you about it now because it doesn't read like much of a dialogue, does it? I've certainly had more riveting discussions in my time. But it turned out to be one of the defining days of my life, because that was the evening I met the woman I was to share my life with and who would become the mother of our six children. Of course I didn't know that then, and I'm sure that if she'd realised she would have run a mile. But the point is this – what seemed like a trivial invitation at the time turned out to have life-changing consequences for us both.

Our twenties is (usually) the time when we make the three most important decisions of our lives: where we live, who we live with, and what we do all day (in other words, our jobs). All three can change over time, but this decade sets our course, and these decisions are often the result of unexpected invitations and conversations. Have you ever heard of chaos theory? One of its more famous ideas is that the flapping of a butterfly's wing could in principle lead to a tornado miles away several weeks later. In the same way, a chance encounter with someone you might not have planned to meet has the potential to change your life. As my friend Neville says, 'You never know when you're being lucky.'

Many people find jobs through others they know, so continuously extending your network makes perfect sense. This means that it's important to open yourself up to social opportunities even if they don't seem like they'll produce a fruitful outcome at the time, because you can't predict which will be the one to pay off. In fact, I met a man recently who told me that every role he'd gained so far had been through a personal introduction and that each of these had, of course, started with a conversation.

One of the best business decisions I ever made began with a random chat. It was an ordinary day in the office back in the spring of 1995, when Sean, one of my technology specialists who still works for REED, came by my office.

'I've an idea,' he announced. My ears pricked up because, as I always say to people, if anyone wants my attention the best way is to say, 'I've an idea.'

'What's your idea, Sean?'

'We should have a website.'

'What's a website?' (It was 1995, remember.)

After Sean had done his best to describe what a website was (imagine how you'd do that for someone who'd never seen one before), I agreed it was worth experimenting with. It turned out that Sean had originally come up with this idea during a conversation with one of our contractors who, when he wasn't working in IT, happened to have a children's party sideline as Pancake the Clown. So we asked Pancake to build a prototype for us. I still have a picture of it now – incredibly clunky by today's standards with buttons that, when clicked on, told you about various aspects of our business. In the corner was a link that said 'Live Jobs'. Our receptionist Kay would type in the jobs to upload them, of which there were just a few at that point, and we added to them over time.

One exciting day, someone applied for a job via the site and was successful. What a moment! Until then, there was no way of discovering jobs in a different part of the country to where you lived. If your home was in Birmingham and you wanted to relocate to Basingstoke, you had no option but to travel to Basingstoke and spend a day registering with recruitment agencies there, or to subscribe to the local paper. We were the first recruitment company to have a website like that, and it was when reed.co.uk was born.

The point of this story is that, at the time, our new website didn't seem like a big deal, but it later became the corner-stone of our business and turned out to be a transformational breakthrough. We became the first UK recruiter to have a presence on the web, and our site became the UK's number one job site and one of the biggest in Europe. In the same way, a chance conversation with a stranger can lead to the most exciting outcomes that you might never have thought were possible. It really is worth giving as much attention as you can to the life-changing nature of invitations and conver-sations, and the new ideas that come with them.

The transformational nature of connecting with other people was also brought home to me recently when my beloved Uncle Jeremy died at the age of eighty-four. I went to his funeral in Birkenhead, Merseyside, where he'd lived for most of his adult life and had worked as a teacher. I was moved and impressed by how packed the church was. He'd been involved with so many aspects of his community – the Sea Cadets, the church, a local art group and orchestra, and more. He wasn't what you'd call a party animal by any means, he was simply interested in people and what they were doing. I came away with the realisation that our lives are enriched by opening ourselves up to connecting with other people, and that it's something we can all do. One thing that I had not expected that sad day was that my sons, who had come with me, left inspired.

HOW TO FIND YOUR PARTIES

When I say 'parties', this is a broad concept. I'm not just talking about music, food and dancing, but about anything that gives you the opportunity to meet people outside your usual social circle. It could be charitable activities, clubs, evening classes, work events or hobbies that involve others. Some people seem to go out all the time, while others stay at home each night. What creates the difference? More often than not it's simply their respective outlooks. The party-goers notice the opportunities around them, go out, meet people, put themselves on those people's social radars, and are then invited to more. Whereas the stay-at-homers focus on who they already know, and don't spot the chances to socialise. It's like they've got their 'party blinkers' on.

Let's have a look at some ways you can broaden your network.

Have interests

I'm being a bit tongue in cheek here because I'm sure you already have some. But do you see them as being an opportunity to meet new people? If you're interested in art, turn up to an exhibition opening. If you're wanting to get fit, see if there's a park run in your area. If you love nothing better than curling up with a good book, find out about book clubs nearby. You'll find that once you start using your interests and hobbies to bring you into contact with like-minded folk, you'll gradually find yourself discovering more and more opportunities. A chance conversation at an exhibition opening, for instance, could lead you to find another one the following month, and there you could happen to meet someone who works in your field. If you're an aspiring artist you might even bump into a professional painter or sculptor, or, better still, a curator or gallery owner. Possibly they'll know about a career opening that's right for you and possibly not, but either way you will have had an interesting time and got to know some interesting people.

Go online

It's never been easier to find people who share your enthusiasms. But I don't mean sitting behind a screen tapping away on social media, I mean using the new generation of meet-up sites to find out what's going on locally to you. Platforms such as Eventbrite and Meetup list what's going on by location and type of event, affording you the chance to sign up to whatever you want. Then you can turn up and get to know people. Of course, social media is a great way of finding out what's going on too, just don't make the mistake of substituting your typing for your presence.

Use your professional networks

Every industry and profession has its associations. See if you can find out what conferences and events are open to someone with your skills and experience – there will be countless people at them who are keen to mingle with others in their field.

Become a volunteer

Offering your time to help with a local (or national) project is an excellent way to get to know people and to showcase your abilities at the same time. If you're great at organising things, for instance, volunteering to coordinate your local team's netball practice sessions would be a good move. Or how about using your marketing know-how to promote a local arts festival?

Recently I had the idea of helping residents in the Grenfell Tower locality of London to develop their careers, because historically there's a high level of social deprivation there. Together with the Kensington and Chelsea Foundation, and supported by Sky TV, we created a programme to put ten people through a four-month computer coding course. These were people who had never had the opportunity to learn anything like this before, but they were willing to give it a go and see what skills they could pick up.

When it was over I watched the students' final presentations and was impressed by how much they'd learned. This was a community initiative relying on the support of local volunteers, and everyone involved found it to be a great way of meeting others and doing something worthwhile. It was a brilliant example of the power of going to parties, but in a way you might not have initially thought of. One of the group, who had been unemployed, now works for REED and is a highly valued member of our team.

Don't wait to be invited

This might seem pushy, but please don't sit around waiting to be asked. Be proactive and find your own events – you'll find that when you turn up it will be worth the effort. In time you can even think of hosting your own 'party'. For instance, if you're part of a local community group you could organise the Christmas pub quiz. Once you start looking for them, there are plenty of social avenues open to you.

HOW TO GET OVER YOURSELF

'But I hate going to parties,' you might be objecting. 'I never know what to say to anyone, and I end up feeling awkward or bored or both.' I sympathise, because I sometimes feel the same way. However, you should still give it a go, because you could open up a new chapter in your life just by saying 'yes' to that one invitation. You don't have to enjoy it; just do it. Your mantra should be, 'At least once a week I'm going to try something social.' The more you step outside your comfort zone the wider that zone will become, and as you become accustomed to chatting to people you'll start to forget your initial discomfort.

When you walk into a room full of people it can feel daunting, but I can guarantee that many others there feel the same as you. They'd love it if someone would come up and introduce themselves. People go to parties to meet people and talk to them, so why shouldn't they want to talk to you? Also, try arriving early so you're not faced with too many strangers at once – I find this works for me.

There's a snowball effect with socialising. At first you feel like an outsider, but then you get to know one person, then another, then another, and in a few weeks or months you'll find yourself being the one to make the introductions for other newbies. Soon you'll be part of the furniture – a regular. And the more confident you feel, the more you'll be confident in yourself, which is the best kind of person you can be.

So don't think too deeply about going to parties, just turn up with the aim of giving something to yourself and others. If, when you return home, you haven't enjoyed it, that's OK. Next time might be better, and nothing's been lost. You might not realise it at the time, but you could have met someone who subsequently becomes instrumental in your life. That person who droned on at you for half an hour non-stop might turn out to know someone, who knows someone, who can help you. Or, if you're unlucky, they might marry your sister – enjoy those entertaining family Christmases! Just think, the idea for your next career move could even come from a chance comment from a fellow party-goer that triggers a train of thought that ends up changing your life. My kids often remind me that I used to tell them, 'If you say "yes" often enough, sooner or later you'll be having an adventure.'

WHAT TO SAY AT PARTIES

It's the worst feeling in the world when you're standing in a room and can't think of what to say, but going to events doesn't have to be like that. All you need is a little preparation. Think of public speaking – almost everyone dreads having to do it, but some of the best speakers I know say they feel like that too. Because they're anxious, they put in the effort to prepare their talks and gradually they became more confident. There's no magic to it.

To help you, here are some sample conversation openers to start you off.

'What have you enjoyed most about today?' Someone once asked me this and I've never forgotten it. When you use it, the person's answer will tell you a lot about them because they're revealing not only what they've been doing but also what they enjoy. This gives you a route into asking more, and then you're off.

'How did you hear about this place?' This is a good one if you're at an interesting venue, and you can carry on chatting about what else goes on there.

'How do you know [the person whose event it is]?' This is a great way of finding out who knows who.

'Did you hear about [x] today?' This could be a story in the news, or some recent event. Their response will tell you what they think about it, and you can take the conversation from there.

'What are you busy with right now?' This can relate either to work or personal life, and gives you the chance to talk about what's preoccupying them at the moment.

You'll notice that all of these conversation openers are questions, showing that you're interested in the other person. So often, and I'm sure you've experienced this, people only talk about themselves. At the end of an evening I've often come away thinking, 'I know everything about you, but you don't know much about me.' When you're interested in others, however, you learn a lot and automatically become *more interesting* because you're a listener. The last time I went to a dinner party I simply asked the woman sitting next to me a series of questions, and when we stood up to go home she said, 'I've had a fascinating time.' I'd barely said a thing. The obvious point to make here is that when you're listening you're learning, and when you're talking you're not.

Try to meet as many people as possible while you're out, and keep an open mind about who you approach. That guy with the strange moustache might look a bit odd, but could be the most fascinating person you meet all month. In this age of social media, people tend to network in their own bubbles, only communicating with those who agree with them. We need to be more open and have conversations with all sorts of people, of all ages and from all walks of life, because we gain so much more information and enrichment from that. It's easy not to do it, but whenever I visit our recruitment offices I make an effort to talk to everyone from the receptionist to the regional director. After all, we're all on the same team and I never know who will come up with the next bright new idea. If I'm not available to everyone, I won't find out.

Once you get into the habit of saying 'yes' to invitations, and even generating your own, you'll find your world becoming richer, more colourful and more interesting. This is a wonderful base from which to explore possibilities around careers and jobs, because you're becoming increasingly open-minded and enthusiastic about the options available to you. At the same time, you're meeting people who might be able to help you (or you them), and expanding your network each time you go to a party. There really isn't much to lose.

WHAT WE COVERED

- You never know when you're about to meet the person who might change your life, so it's important to put yourself in front of as many people as possible.
- Going to parties gives you opportunities to enrich your life and career.
- There are many ways to discover parties to attend, such as following your interests, searching online, using your professional networks, and volunteering.
- Even if you don't feel like going, just do it.
- There are lots of ways to start conversations at parties, and it's easier if you're prepared with a few lines.

AND JUST ASKING . . .

- Have you thought of joining a group activity outside of your normal social circle such as a running club or choir, and if so what might it be?
- What did you get out of the last event you went to, and how could you build on it for next time?

CHAPTER 3

Play Poohsticks

If you ever read the Winnie the Pooh books when you were a kid, the title of this chapter will mean something to you. In *The House at Pooh Corner*, Pooh accidentally invents a game with his friend Eeyore when he drops a fir cone over a bridge. He sees it floating down the river and has the idea of turning it into a competition to see which cone appears under the bridge first. This is how the game of Poohsticks is invented (he swaps cones for sticks when he realises that they're easier to identify). The logic is simple. The stick that lands and stays in the fastest-flowing part of the stream wins, and the one that bobs along on a slower current loses. In a worst-case scenario, it becomes jammed behind a rock or log and never makes it under the bridge at all.

And here's the thing: it's not the sleekest or best-shaped twig that necessarily wins; it's the one that travels the furthest most quickly, using the energy of the stream to its advantage. In the same way, you need to find the fast-flowing water for your career – the sectors and types of job that are just starting to come into high demand. Because you don't have to be the best technologist or the brightest person so long as you locate your career in an area that will carry you further than others. Or, to look at it from the opposite angle, if you're a senior manager who's done extremely well for yourself but you're working in a declining industry, you're not going to go nearly as far as someone who's merely an OK manager in a rapidly growing field.

In my spare time I'm a Master Scuba Diver, a qualification that, as it happens, took me seventeen years longer to achieve than my Master of Business Administration. A few years ago I was diving with my brother-in-law Peter in a balmy, tropical sea off the island of Lombok in Indonesia, scouting for giant clams and turtles, when we rounded a corner of the reef and were instantly surrounded by a huge shoal of fearsome-looking barracuda. I don't know if you've ever seen these fish but they have pointed, fang-like teeth and large jaws, and these ones circled around us as if they didn't want us to escape.

At first it was unnerving, but after a while I became mesmerised by their fluid motion – it was one of the most beautiful and amazing things I'd ever experienced. What could be going on? My question was answered as we swam a little further around the corner of the reef, only to be instantly whisked away by a current of ice-cold water that whooshed us along the reef like a rapid. My mind was swimming faster than my body as I struggled to re-orientate myself. I had no idea what direction I was heading in or if my diving buddy was even with me. That shoal of barracuda now seemed to have been a warning.

Then I remembered my drift-dive training. When you learn to scuba at an advanced level, one of the skills you master is how to cope with fast-flowing water. The trick is not to try to swim against the current because you'll only exhaust yourself. Instead you go along with it, letting it pull you as far as it wants until after a while it gradually evens out. Then you can come to the surface to re-orientate. So I allowed the current to pull me along and even started to find it exhilarating. When it eventually weakened, I swam to the surface and saw that Peter wasn't far away. We signalled to the boat to pick us up. That's when I looked around and was amazed at how far we'd travelled and with so little effort.

In a way, I was like a winning Poohstick that had been tossed from a bridge into a strong current and come out the other side in super-fast time. And this is exactly what can happen to you when you secure a role in an area that will be in high demand for the foreseeable future. You'll see so much more and travel so much further than if you choose still water. That's because fast-flowing sectors represent an abundance of opportunity, with more and more jobs becoming available as they expand. You can grow with them and have a good chance of picking and choosing where you work; there are few better ways of boosting your career than that.

FAST-FLOWING SECTORS

So, what kinds of industries and sectors are the best to explore? They change all the time. When I was a student many of my friends wanted to be management consultants, journalists or investment bankers. Fast-forward to today and I wouldn't call any of these options especially fast flowing, would you? Even management consultancy, which is still a great career if you love it and are good at it, isn't in rapid growth. Instead, areas such as biotech, genetics, machine-learning and robotics are in the ascendant. Which leaves me wishing that I'd paid more attention in my school technology and science classes.

Naturally, what's in growing demand will change from year to year, but as of today here are some of the areas in which I am seeing an increasing number of job opportunities:

- Artificial intelligence
- Biotechnology
- Cybersecurity
- Data management
- Financial technologies (FinTech)
- Green energy and technology
- Medical research
- Mental wellbeing
- Virtual reality

By the time you read this there will have been further changes, but broadly speaking the fastest growing employment sectors at the moment are to do with technology, medical research and renewable energy. Now you may be thinking, 'Well that's all very well, but I'm hopeless at technology – I'm just not that kind of person. When I analysed my preferences at the beginning of this book I came out as being an action-orientated, practical type who loves looking after people and bringing teams together. I can't see myself fitting into any of these areas.' This is an understandable concern and I'll address it in two ways.

First of all, there's no getting away from it, you do have to take into account your passions and preferences when it comes to choosing a career. You'll be unlikely to succeed in any job if you're not a good fit for it. For instance, I'm no good at sitting still – I couldn't do one of those jobs where you're chained to a screen all day. But I do love meeting people and travelling widely, and I'm curious by nature and keen on adventures. So by luck or judgement I've ended up in a career that I'm well suited for as REED is a service business that helps people in various locations and has a continuous need to find better ways of doing things. A perfect psychological match.

However (and this is the next part), please don't despair if you can't see an obvious fit between you and some of these areas of employment, because there's always a way of working yourself in. You can take into account your passions, skills and the things you're good and bad at, and still apply them to many fast-flowing sectors.

Just suppose you love working with people, so the last thing you can see yourself doing is tapping at your keyboard with headphones on while you create the next blockbuster virtual reality game. Gaming companies aren't only in need of programmers, they're also crying out for people with excellent interpersonal skills to help them sell their technology and enable their teams to work more effectively. You could be one of them. Or how about financial services? You might not be a whiz with numbers, but FinTech is a rapidly expanding field that's helping banks and financial institutions to make it easier for their customers to access their money. If you have an adventurous spirit there are multiple start-ups (and larger companies) focused on this sector, and they all need people with diverse skills and outlooks. You could be a customer experience expert, a project manager or an administrator, and still find a home in them.

If you look hard enough, there's fast-flowing water to suit almost anyone. As I sit in my office working on this book, I can look out over the floor and see technologists, customer specialists, data scientists and my marketing team. They're all focused on one thing – making our business more effective – but they each have their own different skills, experiences and drives. Taking myself as an example again, at school I wasn't particularly good at science but my interest in technology has never been due to the technology itself. What I am interested in is how technology can be used to give people a better experience. That's what matters to me. What I add to our own tech, therefore, is the human factor. When you match your strengths, talents and interests to what's in demand, it's like adding a turbo boost to your personal Poohstick. This will propel you through the water into a winning position, with minimal effort on your part.

FAST-FLOWING JOBS

This leads me on to the fact that even in sectors that aren't in growth, some of the roles within them may still be. I've recently hired a Customer Experience Officer, or CXO. A year ago I'd not heard of one, but in common with many businesses today our special focus is on putting the experience of our customers right at the centre of our operations. The rise of digital has made it easier for organisations to interact quickly and accurately with their customers, which has led their expectations to rise as a result. Now companies have to put an increased emphasis on satisfying and retaining the people they serve. This means that customer management roles are becoming more important, and people like my new CXO are in hot demand.

I was talking to someone not long ago who told me that in recent years jobs with the title of DevOps have also taken off. They're based on managing the development of technology within organisations in a way that links with how that technology will be used, often within the context of cloud-hosting services. The roles frequently pay six-figure salaries. These jobs barely even existed two years ago, but cloud computing has exploded, creating a growth in allied jobs in its wake. This just shows how having an awareness of emerging spaces when you're thinking about what to do next can be invaluable.

By the way, fast-flowing doesn't have to mean glamorous. In fact, careers in areas such as music or TV are so competitive that you'll find succeeding in them to be like pushing water uphill. Even if the river isn't sparkling, if it's moving along at pace that's all that matters.

HOW TO SPOT THE FAST-FLOWING WATER

Finding the fast-flowing water for your career is like water divining – easy to say and hard to do. After all, you're seeking out the sectors and job titles that not everyone else knows about, and when you look at the surface of the water you can't always see where the current is. You can't rely on copying your friends (unless you have some savvy ones – in which case, lucky you), or even scanning the internet, because the last thing you want is to follow the herd. The roles that appear repeatedly are the ones that pose the stiffest competition, and you want to target the less obvious opportunities that everyone else isn't seeking out. This isn't an easy thing to advise you on, but there are three main ways to find your fast-flowing water.

Be curious and keep an open mind

Talk to people (remember the parties you're going to?). Ask questions. Subscribe to blogs about random topics. Notice things, like what's going on in your local area. What's changing? What's new? What's exciting? For instance, at REED we're always on the lookout for new clients for our recruitment business, and we like to find ones that are in fast-growing sectors because they'll be looking to hire more people. We carry out research to find them, some of which is desk-based but much of it involves conversations and local knowledge, such as noticing if a firm moves into a new office development. Why are they expanding? In the same way, keeping alive to what's changing and happening around you can unlock a host of interesting career opportunities.

Consider your strengths

Here's where looking in the mirror pays off. What are you good at? What do you enjoy? And how could this combination of factors lead you to your own fast-flowing river? As an example, if finance is something that excites you, you're not limited to jobs in traditional financial institutions (which aren't in growth). Instead, ask yourself what are the fastest-moving segments of finance and apply your talents to them. In London, for instance, you'll find one of the world's central bases for innovation in FinTech, with many new companies starting up and hiring in that space. Even if you work for a large investment bank rather than a new technology start-up, it will have some business streams that are moving more rapidly than others. Which areas are busy at the moment? What departments might be hiring because they're growing? Finance doesn't become a bad area to go into because of the global financial crisis; money still makes the world go round and if you're in the thick of it you will have a great career.

Be lucky

When I found myself making my drift-dive it wasn't planned, but I made the most of it when it happened. In the same way, it's interesting how seemingly randomly you can find your fast-flowing water. Taking the time to talk to diverse people on a regular basis will make you luckier than your neighbour who stays at home with Deliveroo every night because you'll receive lots of information that they miss out on. The key thing with luck is to recognise it when you see it. Don't ignore that passing comment from someone about an interesting role or a new industry that's taking off; follow up on it and find out more. You never know if it could be the tip-off that makes the difference.

STEADY SECTORS

There are many roles within what I call calmer waters, that will always be needed – at least for the foreseeable future. They're not fast-flowing, but they're still valuable because they're not here today and gone tomorrow. If you base your career in one of these you'll always be in demand, just in a different way than if you were riding the rapids. Instead of having the potential to flow with your industry you'll be a 'steady eddy', always needed and always useful. Given that a job is a problem to be solved, it's no bad thing to focus on what issues will always need dealing with no matter what.

Think of teaching, for example. If you're a teacher, you'll always be busy and (if you enjoy it) have a very fulfilling job. While the nature of teaching might change over the years, it will be forever required in some form or other. Recently at REED we worked with schools, employers and career guidance teams to discover what organisations most want from the next generation of school leavers. They said that mindset and personal skills, such as willingness to learn, motivation, team spirit, confidence and having something to say, were more important to them than task-related skills. These are the qualities a good teacher can encourage, and they can't be learned from a computer, only from a living, breathing person who has their students' best interests at heart. So if you're keen on teaching, just do it and don't worry about whether it's fast-flowing or not. It will always be a promising career one way or another.

What kinds of jobs and sectors are steady eddies? I can't list them all, but here are some to start you thinking. As you can see they tend to be based in the physical rather than the technological world, because even though our lives are increasingly being played out online we still have bodies and material needs that need catering for. They're not necessarily the most glamorous fields, but they can still provide a rewarding array of job opportunities that withstand the test of time.

- Caring and medical professions such as physiotherapy, nursing and home-care (think of our ageing population)
- Catering and hospitality
- Education
- Medicine
- Sales (we still like to buy from people)
- Skilled trades such as plumbing and building houses
- Waste disposal

There's an interesting thing that careers and comedy have in common: they both require excellent timing. Not only that, but, like a comedian, your challenge is to put together unexpected combinations of thoughts and ideas because originality can be your strongest card. It might seem a little daunting to jump into fast-flowing water, but don't be afraid to do it. When I was whisked away by that current on my scuba-diving trip it was strange at first, but it turned out to be a lot of fun and something I'd love to experience again. I learned that the only currents that are really dangerous are the ones that go deep down into the sea, so if you find your sector or role to be one that's in rapid decline, it may be time to shoot to the side and come up for some air. Finding the fast-flowing water should be your number one responsibility if you want to win at Poohsticks.

WHAT WE COVERED

- When you locate your career in fast-growing industries or sectors, you'll be more likely to progress quickly, and with less effort, than if you choose a declining industry.
- The same goes for job roles that are in growth, even if they're in mature sectors.
- You can always find a way of matching your talents and skills to fast-flowing industries, even if it's not the most obvious option.
- Finding sectors and job roles that are in the early stages of growth isn't easy, and if it were, everyone would be doing it. Keep your eyes and ears open and talk to people.
- Certain areas will always be in demand, even if they're not in growth.

AND JUST ASKING . . .

- Have you identified a fast-flowing sector that appeals to you?

- Can you see a link between what you learned by 'looking in the mirror' and the types of industries that would enable your career to take off?

CHAPTER 4

Be Selfish

This might sound like a strange analogy, but in a career context I think of selfishness as being a bit like cholesterol: there's a good and a bad kind. The bad is when you only think about yourself and what you want, ignoring other people's needs. The good is when you make doing work you love a priority, because when you're in a job you enjoy you'll have energy for it and want to keep improving. Both you and your organisation will benefit, and this is what I mean by being 'sustainably' selfish – it's the kind of self-interest that pays dividends all round. You can also look at it from the opposite angle. Working in a role that saps your energy and makes you feel low will eventually damage your health. It isn't good for your boss either, any more than using up the earth's resources too quickly is sustainable for the future of the planet. Your enthusiasm for life and work is too precious to waste, so let's work out where it should be best spent.

Of course, we all have a fair amount of 'bad' selfishness in us – we're only human after all. Being candid, I know that I'm quite a selfish person and I'm sure my wife would agree! But I see being a bit selfish sometimes as a necessary part of doing a great job. I have a strong purpose in life that's related to my work, so sometimes I find myself brushing aside distractions that get in my way, so I am able to make my aims a priority. I hope you have a drive to achieve something too, but also that you realise that selfishness doesn't have to be a negative thing.

There's a current view that our increasing consumption of social media and self-help books is encouraging an attitude of looking after number one. For me, this is more about self-awareness than selfishness. Also, 'good' selfishness – the sustainable kind – can balance out the bad kind, because focusing on what you want can make the difference between performing at a so-so level and becoming a star at what you do. It's energising and satisfying to love your day.

So this chapter is about the importance of finding work you really want to do and doing it in a way you enjoy, because you'll perform so much better at it than if you don't. As the Chinese philosopher Confucius said, 'Choose a job you love, and you will never have to work a day in your life.'

WHAT GOES WRONG WHEN YOU'RE NOT SUSTAINABLY SELFISH?

Because the notion of selfishness is so loaded with negativity (and rightly so if it's unsustainable), it's worth exploring the downsides of *not* doing a job you love before we go any further. Do you dread going into work, and catch yourself glancing at the clock every half-hour until you can go home? Do you live for the next holiday? I feel for you if so.

Measuring out your time by counting the weeks until you can make your escape is no way to live at all.

I appreciate that you may be doing a job because you need the money and there's no other option right now, and that's understandable. Or you might have found yourself in a role that's well paid but unsatisfying. As long as you're making a conscious decision about it that's your choice, but are either of these scenarios sustainable in the long run? Often I come across people in these kinds of situations and they seem to talk a lot about early retirement, but even when they retire they aren't always happy because what they really wanted all along was to feel fulfilled. Or maybe they carry on with their work because they don't know what else to do. A friend of mine, John, has been working in finance for many years and says that if he had his time again he would never have touched the field. Like many people in his fifties, he now feels it's too late to change (it isn't, but it does become harder the older you are).

As for money, in my experience of talking to countless people who enjoy their work, it's rarely the most important contributing factor. These individuals tell me they want to make a difference, witness the impact they've created, and feel rewarded by it. The same can be true in reverse. When people are in work that's unfulfilling, they find themselves falling into the way of thinking that there's no point changing it because there are no other options. It's dispiriting, isn't it? And this can lead to burn-out. We tend to think of 'burning out' as being applicable to high-powered jobs, in which people at the top of organisations feel overwhelmed by their responsibilities and workload. But the reality is that it can affect anyone, because when you're constantly expending your energy on something you find unpleasant, boring, or isolating, it takes its toll on your physical and emotional health.

The job I least enjoyed in my life was a two-month stint aged seventeen as a cemetery worker beside the River Thames in Old Windsor. I had to level the graves and maintain the grounds in all weathers – it was cold, miserable and boring because I was on my own. Luckily it paid well and didn't last for long as I was only doing it between school and university, but I dread to think how I'd have felt if it had been a permanent role. It taught me how easy it is, when you're unhappy with your work, to feel that you're stuck in it with no way out because you're not seeing the wood for the trees. Especially when you need the money and may be struggling to make ends meet, it can be hard to lift your head up high enough to view the landscape of opportunities around you.

I hope by now that you can see what a problem it is to do work you dislike – it's certainly not sustainable in the long term if you want to be happy, healthy and a pleasure to be around. With that in mind, let's consider the key elements of a worthwhile job.

FEEL-GOOD JOB FACTORS

Each December, if you were to walk through the doors of the Ritz Hotel on London's Piccadilly around midday, you'd see a group of excited REED colleagues heading towards the private dining area. They're attending a celebratory lunch for everyone who's been with us for a milestone era – this could be ten, twenty, twenty-five, thirty and, in some cases, as many as forty years. In fact, last December we held seven such lunches for a total of 140 people. At the beginning of the meal I like to ask what's kept these people in their jobs for so long, and while the answers naturally vary from person to person they all follow a common set of themes. These are the areas I'll explore here, and they group into nine feel-good fundamentals.

Doing the kind of work you enjoy and are good at

The big one – this is the core of being sustainably selfish. Your job must suit your passions, values and purpose, and make the most of your natural talents. When you do work you're well suited to, you'll find yourself making an impact with minimal effort, and that will be recognised by those around and above you. This will lead to you being well rewarded because companies will want to keep you, others will want to hire you, and many will want to promote you. This is due to the energy, application and enthusiasm you'll be bringing to your work each day. Play to your strengths.

Getting on with your colleagues

If you've experienced the torture of spending a whole weekend with relatives you don't get on with, you can only imagine how awful it is to work five days a week with colleagues you dislike. Some people, however, are lucky enough to make good friends at work and these relation-ships can last a lifetime. Even if you don't forge any close personal friendships, it makes all the difference to your day if you can turn to a colleague for support when you're having a difficult time, or pass the time of day with a joke or a story. And when your team is well balanced in terms of abilities and talents, you can see your own efforts being multiplied.

Having opportunity and variety

Being bored and feeling stale are inherently dissatisfying states to be in. When you have the chance to stretch yourself by taking on a new project, or are motivated to go for a promotion because you feel you have the chance to progress, you'll want to stay in your job and work harder at it. It's important to find a place where you're able to learn, grow and stay interested.

Feeling able to make a difference

In his book *Bullshit Jobs: A Theory*, anthropologist David Graeber explains how German psychologist Karl Groos first discovered that babies find it joyfully satisfying when they first discover that they can have an effect on something, regardless of whether it benefits them or not. Witness an infant's delight when it knocks over a tower of bricks and you see his point. Groos called this 'the pleasure at being the cause', and it's something that we carry with us all our lives. It's human to want to make a difference – to be able to say, 'I did that.' Whether it be an improvement to a current process or the introduction of something totally new, your job must offer you this opportunity if it's to be sustainable.

Doing meaningful work

A while ago I went through a phase of running marathons, taking part in the London, Paris and New York events. The most helpful piece of advice I was given was to think about one person who was important to me during each of the twenty-six miles. It was a brilliant technique, because not only did the time fly by but it also gave the experience so much meaning – it was thought-provoking, rewarding and enjoyable (not normally emotions you'd associate with running for hours on end). I learned that a marathon is less about what goes on with your legs and more about what's happening in your head. In the same way, if you feel your work is important and worthwhile, you'll be likely to enjoy it no matter what it is. It could be sweeping the streets, caring for elderly people, or running a business – these jobs are all sustainable if you recognise that there's a purpose to them.

Having fun

This is one of the most important aspects of work for me – to have a laugh. I'm known for my jokes around the office and sometimes people complain, but I always think they'd rather groan at my jests than be serious all the time. I can't stand the thought of not being light-hearted at work because it's part of what makes it sustainable. Having a sense of humour helps you to cope when you have a bad day, otherwise it would be so demoralising. And people who make others feel good are popular to have around.

Location, location, location

Whenever I interview someone for a job I always take into account where they live. I tell them I don't want them having to do a long journey, and when they ask why, I reply, 'I'd rather you were happy at home or happy at work, rather than wasting your time shuttling between the two. There's not much value in commuting.' Although you can certainly fill the time travelling to and from work with some meaningful activities, it soon becomes tiring and a chore. Do you really want to spend three hours a day on a train, bus or motorway?

Being able to be yourself

There are some who say the 'bring-your-whole-self-to-work' movement has gone too far, but I think there's a lot in it. Being yourself and being sustainably selfish are closely linked, because if you're true to yourself in temperament, talent and skills, you're more likely to progress and succeed than if you don't feel at home in your work environment. You're also less likely to burn out if you're not constantly trying to pretend to be someone you're not.

Finding a culture that's a fit

Underpinning all these fundamentals is the culture in which you work, which is often created by the founder or leader of your organisation and practised by the people who work in it. Every workplace has a different culture, just as every person has a different character. Unless you're the head honcho, please don't waste your energy on trying to change your company culture because you won't succeed. As management guru Peter Drucker once said, 'Culture eats strategy for breakfast.' What he meant was that if a strategy doesn't fit the culture it will never work. Similarly, if your personality, outlook and values clash with the culture of the place you spend your time in, you'll be the one to lose out.

HOW TO BE SUSTAINABLY SELFISH

Hopefully you're sold on the idea of loving your work, but how do you put it into practice? If you're already in a job you can start by asking yourself the question 'Do I enjoy it?' If your answer isn't an unequivocal 'yes', you should do some re-examining of your situation. And if you're not in work at the moment, then you're free to start with a clean slate. Here's how to go about it.

Revisit yourself

Using the increased self-awareness you're developing by now, ask yourself what are the things you love to do. What sort of people would you like to do them with? Who do you receive positive energy from? And what kinds of activities give you that energy as well? Then construct your working day and life around those people and things that – selfishly – you like.

Branch out

Where could you find the kind of job that gives you as many of those nine feel-good fundamentals as possible?

You must have some friends or neighbours who seem happier than others – why not ask them where they work and if they'd recommend the place? So often the best source of insight is under our nose. Also, bear in mind that some organisations reward people who introduce successful applicants to the firm. One of my daughters, for instance, gained a role in a US technology company due to a friend who referred her and who gained a substantial bonus as a result. That organisation now has two happy people working for it, and didn't have to struggle to find them. If you know people who seem to love their workplace and you think you might too, ask if they'll introduce you to someone – there may be something in it for both of you.

If you're already in a job and not enjoying it, there are also options internally. Is there a way you could establish yourself more effectively so you can progress the way you'd like? Could you bring yourself to the attention of people who could support and develop you? The rest of this book will give you lots of ideas for how you can do this.

And, finally, don't forget online research, especially the workplace-review site Glassdoor. Good companies put energy into creating a great place to work, and are focused on making their teams feel welcome because they want a diverse, dynamic workforce. It's important to them that they have talented people who feel they belong. Many organisations talk about diversity and inclusion but I prefer inclusion and then diversity. Because the most important factor to me is whether people feel included as part of the family when they join our business. Diversity of backgrounds is important, but the starting point is that we have a culture of belonging. Feeling at home in a job is part of what makes it sustainable.

Invest in some self-care

There's nothing more sustainably selfish than making sure that you keep fit and healthy, and also that you have enough sleep. This has a huge bearing on how easy you'll find it to sustain the marathon that a career represents. For instance, I go to the gym on Tuesdays and Fridays, and because I know that I won't have time after work I do it between 6 and 7 a.m. It's the one part of the day I can guarantee that no one will be bothering me with appointments or phone calls. Some people think I'm nuts, but I enjoy it and I do it for selfish reasons. If you want to be seen as someone with energy and drive it's usually a given that you have good health, because otherwise the aura you exude might harm your prospects and those of your organisation. It's sustainable for both parties if you're fit and well.

Control your attention

How you manage your time is something you should pay close attention to. When people start filling up your diary and you end up in countless meetings that are of little benefit to you, it's time to set some boundaries. My starting point, for instance, is that no meeting should last more than half an hour, which means that my first decision is whether I'm prepared to commit that amount of time to the person in question. For me, that's manageable.

You might be wondering how you can achieve this if you're a junior member of staff. Surely you can't refuse to go to meetings or be involved in work that you think is of no value? You might find it a challenge but everyone can control something, and when you approach your job with the mindset of someone who has a say in how you spend your day you'll be amazed at what you can change. You also have an influence over how you respond to things in general. If someone is having a negative effect on your day, for instance, you can choose to ignore them or, alternatively, to do something about it. This makes your job sustainable, because you'll be less likely to want to give up on things when you know the power lies within you.

I hope you can see now that being sustainably selfish is not just about pursuing happiness on a personal level, but about creating a situation in which you feel positive about your work, and your workplace therefore feels equally positive about you. Both sides benefit in this happy equation.

WHAT WE COVERED

- Being sustainably selfish means doing work you enjoy so that both you and your organisation benefit.
- When you're not sustainably selfish in your job, you're likely to burn out.
- Although money is important it's rarely the main reason most people do a job – you have to enjoy it too.

- There are nine feel-good fundamentals for sustainable work: doing what you enjoy, having good colleagues, having the opportunity to try new things, being able to make a difference, doing work with meaning, having fun, working close to home, being yourself and finding a well-fitting culture.
- You can build a sustainably selfish career by cultivating self-awareness, talking to people about opportunities at great workplaces, looking after yourself physically, and managing your time and responses in a healthy way.

AND JUST ASKING ...

- Out of the nine feel-good fundamentals, which is the most important to you?
- When you think of the jobs you've done in the past, which did you most enjoy and why?

CHAPTER 5

Kick-Start Some Good Habits and Kick Out Some Bad Ones

'Early to bed, early to rise, work like hell, and advertise,' said Ted Turner, founder of US news channel CNN. He was being asked for the secrets of his success, but what he was actually talking about was habits – those things we do every day that create our lives. Because habits dictate what we think, how we spend our time and therefore what we achieve. What is habitual tends to get done, and if it leads to a worthwhile outcome is excellent, but if it doesn't can end up in an unhealthy scenario in which we never reach our goals. Think of your habits as the foundation stones of your career.

Because habits are such powerful creatures, it's worth learning how to cultivate a life in which helpful ones are the order of the day. To be a habit-challenger, you need to be the kind of person who's willing to question what you do and why you do it. It's terribly easy to slip into habits at work, both good and bad, so this chapter is about how to develop as many positive ones as possible while reducing the negatives.

HABITS YOU WANT TO HAVE

Habits are pretty simple in that they fall into two camps: those you want to have and those you don't. In my experience of managing and leading large numbers of people, I've come across all sorts of ways of working and seeing the world, and have learned that there are a few key habits you need if you want to be the best version of yourself.

Being cheerful

Craig Donaldson, CEO of Metro Bank, says that he never hires someone who doesn't smile within the first two minutes of a job interview. That's because positive people are uplifting to be around, and every boss wants a level of productivity and happiness in their workplace. Critical to this are both having a healthy lifestyle and getting enough sleep – if you come in boot-faced in the morning because you've only had four hours' kip the night before, you'll be a mood-hoover not an energiser. It certainly won't help you to succeed in your career, and nor will you enjoy it. Smiling and laughing several times a day are therefore good habits to have.

Being an improver

For many years, I've been fascinated by the Japanese business philosophy of Kaizen (which means 'improvement'). It involves everyone in a company, from the shop-floor worker to the CEO, making small improvements all the time. I've observed that the companies that apply this way of thinking are usually the most successful ones, because hundreds and thousands of incremental enhancements will lead to amazing outcomes. So a good habit is to be continually seeking ways of doing things better.

Reviewing regularly

Another helpful routine is to ask yourself at the end of each day (maybe on your commute home), 'What have I learned today? And what did I contribute?' I always carry a notebook with me and when I think of something I can action I write it down. At the moment it's open on my desk and I can see that I've written three to-dos (which I've completed) and some points from a meeting yesterday which I'd like to follow up on. I even keep my New Year's resolutions in it, just for fun. One of them was to write this book.

I have a habit each year of setting annual objectives for my company, myself and our family. This helps me to think about my life and opportunities in the long term, which would be easy to forget or ignore if I didn't make a point of regularly reviewing where I'm at.

Rising early

When I went to business school in the United States I discovered how much earlier students seemed to get up over there, so I decided to follow suit. Instead of starting at 9 a.m. as I would have done at home, I joined my study group at 7.20 in the morning and was sitting in my first class by 8.30. It's a habit I've kept ever since, because I achieve so much more when I begin the day in a timely manner.

Your most productive time might not be first thing – you may be more of a night owl, in which case you're at your best later in the day or in the evening. If you can, try to find a career in which you can work the hours that suit your own body clock.

Keeping healthy

At REED we help a lot of people with smoking cessation and weight management, and we can quickly see how much happier and more productive they are when they improve their lifestyles. You don't have to be a tobacco addict or a couch potato to develop healthier habits, though; we can all get into a better groove. It's amazing how losing a few pounds or being able to run for the bus without gasping for breath can put a spring in your step, and this will also give you energy for pursuing your career.

Getting on with things

A great habit to have at work is to prioritise the items on your to-do list that you're least looking forward to – that way you quickly clear your desk of dismal or difficult tasks, removing any anxiety associated with them at the same time. This will lead you to feel more cheerful, clear the way to accomplishing better things and encourage you to focus.

Being open-minded and curious

One of the most interesting habits to cultivate is that of listening and looking without prejudice. I'm not referring to being unbiased about people's gender, race and so on (that's a given) but I am talking about taking it a step further by being completely dispassionate about them. Because the more open-minded you are when you view the world around you, the more you'll notice and the less likely you'll be to jump to unhelpful and habitual conclusions. Many job opportunities have been overlooked because the potential applicant didn't 'see' them – they had their habit blinkers on. Keeping a curious outlook, on the other hand, can lead to all sorts of new and exciting discoveries.

Being grateful

Acknowledging and expressing your appreciation for what life has to offer keeps you aware of the positives, which in turn boosts your energy and encourages you to be aware of new opportunities. It also endears you to people because there's nothing more rewarding than being thanked by someone, and we don't do it often enough. My brother always rings our mum on a Sunday evening. It is a habit he has cultivated because he wants to show his appreciation for her, and it goes down well. Maybe I should take a leaf out of his book.

As an aside, when I shared an early version of this book with some trusted colleagues a couple of them said, 'James, these are *your* good habits. Mine are different.' This underlines the intensely personal nature of habits. So I asked them what they would add and received some strong answers. One said that being polite to everyone they met, showing empathy and remembering things about people were important to them. Another said that they always tried to be present in company. A third stressed the value of his military training: making your bed at the start of every day, showering morning and evening, wearing a clean shirt and always using a deodorant. He at least will never be on the wrong end of an awkward 'personal hygiene' conversation!

This might be a good time for you to consider your own good habits. List the first three that come to mind:

_____

_____

_____

Are there some more that you would like to add? Why not list them here:

_____

_____

_____

WHEN A GOOD HABIT BECOMES A BAD ONE

Can you smile too much? Is it possible to be too open-minded? Could rising early become unhelpful if you don't get enough sleep? Good habits can turn into bad ones if they're taken to extremes. Being cheerful is great for you and everyone around you, but things are seldom perfect and it would be complacent and disingenuous to think or behave otherwise. Keeping an open outlook is the key to spotting opportunities, but you need to exercise judgement as well – sometimes a little scepticism can make the difference between having an exciting ride and being taken for one. And if rising at the crack of dawn only leads to burnout and exhaustion, it's obviously not a good thing. So treat your good habits with respect – cherish them but be aware that they will only be helpful if well applied.

HABITS YOU WANT TO AVOID

In the spirit of being positive, I'm keeping my list of bad habits to a minimum. Many, of course, are simply the opposites of the ones above, but there are three additional performance-shrinkers that deserve a special mention.

Complaining

This might seem to be the complete opposite of being cheerful, but there's more to it than that. Most people sympathise if you're a bit under the weather or feeling low because you're going through a tough few weeks, *as long as you're not always moaning about it*. One of my colleagues went on a two-week cruise to the Caribbean and came back to the office with an unseasonal suntan. 'Had a good time?' I asked enviously. 'Yes,' he replied. 'But you wouldn't believe it – I caught a cold on the plane on the way home.' There was no mention of the exciting things he'd seen and done, just a reference to the sniffles. Was I sympathetic? No, I wasn't.

It's not hard to see how a grumpy, miserable moaner will find their career more of a struggle than someone who wins support and encouragement by noticing the brighter side of events. I'm always amused by the expression that by the time you reach forty your face is your own fault.

Being addicted to things

When we think about the word 'addiction' we tend to associate it with drugs, alcohol, tobacco and other things that can be harmful when indulged in to excess. But are these really habits? I believe so – they're just extreme versions of other routines we slip into, but they have more harmful consequences. I'm quite an addictive person myself and over the years have had to severely curtail my consumption of both alcohol and tobacco, so I understand what it's like to rely on them. I've found that if I can channel my energy and drive into something more purposeful, it's a lot more productive and I'm a lot happier. People sometimes say that I become easily obsessed with things, but I can live with that and thankfully my family are good at organising distractions for me.

Apart from anything else, being addicted to something, whether it be gambling, exercise or fast food, is no fun. I can see Victoria Station in London from my window right now, and the solitary smokers hanging around outside in the January drizzle don't look like they're having a great time. If they were to kick the habit they'd likely find themselves with more confidence and energy, both of which are serious career-boosters.

Being a couch potato

When you're in your twenties you can sometimes get away with not exercising too much, but the older we grow the more important it is to fit it into our daily lives so that we have the energy to do well at work and at home. You'll sleep soundly and come into the office with a bounce and a sparkle if you're exercising regularly. I remember hearing that when you reach forty you'll either be fit or fat, so I try hard to make sure it's the former.

You've listed some of your good habits, now's a chance to be brutally honest with yourself and to declare some of your bad ones. List the first three that come to mind:

1. _____

2. _____

3. _____

Now reflect for a moment. What are the consequences of these habits, for you and for people you care about? Choose three:

1. _____

2. _____

3. _____

THE COMPANY YOU KEEP

Motivational speaker Jim Rohn once said that we're the average of the five people we spend most time with. That's because, even if we don't realise it, the company we keep has a huge influence over the habits we develop – we take our cues from our closest friends, family and colleagues.

I mentioned earlier that I gave up smoking, and it was moving to the US to study that did it for me. I was quite a heavy smoker, working my way through twenty or thirty a day, but none of my fellow students were similarly addicted. I even noticed that while British pubs stank of tobacco in those days, the ones in Boston smelled of shampoo instead (big hair was the thing at the time). I decided to quit, and while it took some willpower it was a lot easier than it would have been at home, simply because none of my friends were smoking as well.

I also became fitter while I was there. On my first day returning from class I was surprised to see joggers weaving along the pavement with tracksuits and headbands on. What could this be? I'd never seen anything like it before. Back in London a drink in the pub was the accepted after-work activity – no one went jogging. Gradually I started to see the benefit in taking regular exercise, and as my classmates were also doing it I thought I may as well join them. By the time I came home I was a whole lot fitter.

I don't want to be overly puritanical about advising you on who you choose to spend time with, because naturally they will be the people you most care about or who you work closely with. There may not be a lot of choice in the matter in any case. But just be aware of how you'll be picking up their good and bad habits. When you can see how this process works you can choose to associate more with those you admire, confident that their positive energy will rub off on you.

YOUR GROWTH MINDSET

Habits, no matter what kind they are, have one thing in common: they all begin and end in our minds, and this is where your mindset comes in. In my book *Put Your Mindset to Work*, I explored the concept of the growth mindset that psychologist Carol Dweck first highlighted. Through her research, she discovered that if you credit your successes purely to being naturally good at things you'll tend to assume that there's a ceiling on what you can achieve. After all, if ability is innate there's not a lot you can do to change it. But if you believe that your own efforts lead to improvement, and that you can always do better, you'll be more likely to work at upping your game. In my book I suggested that people try what I call micro challenges to prove this works for them. For instance, when you next board a plane, instead of flicking through the usual glossy magazines ask yourself what you want to learn in your time in the air and load your carry-on bag with useful reading material instead.

Vala Afshar, the Chief Digital Evangelist at US company Salesforce, is a great dispenser of wisdom on Twitter and I often enjoy reading what he has to say. One of my favourites is his realisation that 'learning to learn, and changing yourself, is a superpower'. It's worth asking yourself: how can I make things better? How can I use my short time on this earth to improve someone else's situation?

Our brains love to follow the same old routine day in and day out, and this reinforces our habits, so it can take an effort to think about life afresh. But it's incredibly worthwhile when you do.

HOW TO IDENTIFY AND CHANGE
YOUR HABITS

Almost by definition, your habits are hard to identify because you carry them out unthinkingly – they're deeply ingrained in your behaviour. Think about your routine when you get up in the morning, for instance. If you're like many people, you brush your teeth, have a shower, get dressed, make yourself a coffee, and pop some bread in the toaster. You then leave home at a set time, taking the same route that you did yesterday, until you arrive at your destination and start your job. There's nothing wrong with that – in fact, a few habits and routines can ease us through life – but it's likely that you do it all without thinking. It's only when you start to dissect it that you realise how habitual it has become.

Emotional habits are even trickier to spot because you can't see them as clearly as behavioural ones. If you tend to frown as you walk into the office because you're worried about the day ahead, you might not realise you're doing it. And if you routinely put off doing your admin because you feel daunted by it, you eventually become used to that pile of papers teetering on the edge of your desk. Behind every action (or lack of one) there's a feeling, and behind that feeling there's a thought. Your task is to identify that thought so that you can decide if this is a habit you want to change or one you want to cultivate.

You might start by asking people who love you what your good and bad habits are. Then, using the suggestions that they provide, have a go at identifying some on your own. Ask yourself if you're generally a cheerful person, for instance, or whether you consider yourself healthy and fit, and see if anything tallies with what your loved ones have told you. You can also cast your mind back to comments people have made about you, although you'll need to bear in mind that you're more likely to remember the negative than the positive – that just seems to be the way we're made.

Another technique is to spend a week recording all your activities and how long they take, right down to how many minutes you spend scrolling through social media on your phone (some phones can tell you that), or how long it takes you to complete a task at work. You'll be amazed at how this sheds light on your habits because, as I said at the beginning, habits are what shape your day. You could even add up these times to give yourself an annual tally.

MAKING THE CHANGE

It's best to see the process of change as replacing a bad habit with a more positive one, in a systematic way. Let's break it down into three simple steps.

Step 1: pinpoint your bad habits

Use the tips above to identify which habits you want to kick out. There will be plenty I'm sure, but don't worry about them all, just list the three that will make the most significant difference to your career.

Step 2: work out what drives the habits

We have our habits for a reason: they give us rewards. For instance, you might routinely check your emails first thing and then find yourself becoming sucked into a vortex of discussions which eat up the most productive hour of your day. Whether you realise it or not, you do this because there's a benefit to you. What could that benefit be? Is it that emailing makes you feel connected with people, or that you're putting off doing something more difficult, or that it's a way of cranking your brain into gear first thing? If it's connection you desire, you could limit your messages to people you actively need to communicate with and leave the rest until later. If procrastination is your reward, recognising the activity for what it is will go a long way towards changing it. This is when willpower comes into play, because when you prioritise the task that you're putting off and you do it day after day, you'll start to experience a *different* reward: the satisfaction of a job well done. And if it's waking yourself up and getting your brain into gear that your email routine gives you, why not listen to a podcast or read a book on the way to work instead? Then you can spring into action the minute you arrive.

Step 3: make the change

Now you have your three habits you want to change, and you know why you do them and what you want to do instead, make a conscious decision to make that shift. Say it to yourself: 'I'm going to stop visiting the workplace vending machine to buy chocolate and bring in fruit instead.

And to give myself the reward I'm after, which I now realise is partly the enjoyment I gain from getting up from my desk and having a walk, I'll wander around and have a chat to my colleagues while I'm munching my apple.'

Sounds easy, doesn't it? I'm not going to pretend it will always be as simple as this. But be reasonable with yourself and take small steps – you're unlikely to become a bad-habit-free person overnight. When you slip up you can tell yourself that tomorrow is another day. After all, the reason that habits are difficult to change is that they're *meant* to be – our brains love the grooves created by repetitive actions and thoughts because they make things easy. They're a bit like the tracks through the grass that a farmer creates as he walks the same route through his fields each day. When he changes direction, he has to do it for a while before the new path unfolds and the old one gradually disappears. Some people say it takes thirty days to change a habit, but I think it can be far longer than that.

It's also worth noticing those around you who are role models for change. Many people who've become addicted to substances or harmful activities do an amazing job of moving away from them towards healthier lifestyles. Their success is ultimately the result of a series of choices they've made, one after the other. By changing their habits, they've changed their lives.

We make choices all the time. What will we eat? Where shall we go? Who will we talk to? A habit is a choice like any other, it's just that we don't necessarily see it like that. But all decisions have consequences, and we can decide to change our habits just like anything else in life. It's up to us.

WHAT WE COVERED

- Habits are powerful because they dictate what we think and do, day after day.
- Your good habits give you energy and positivity, whereas your bad ones sap your strength and remove opportunities from your path.
- Some good habits are being cheerful, carrying out regular self-reviews, rising early, keeping healthy, avoiding procrastination, being open-minded and being grateful.
- Some bad habits are being a complainer, becoming an addict, and not taking enough exercise.
- Changing a habit is a three-step process: identify the ones you want to change, work out what rewards you gain from them, and replace them with ones you would like to have instead.

AND JUST ASKING . . .

- What's one good habit that you'd like to start?
- And which bad habit will you try to stop?

CHAPTER 6

Pick Your Targets

When I go to the gym I wear a top with a slogan that I love: 'To score, you have to have goals.' This sums up the value of targets for me, because to go places in your career you have to know what you desire in the first place. After all, football wouldn't be much of a game without the net, would it?

One of the reasons why targets are so important is because they're a natural part of life. When you were a child your parents decided them on your behalf – you were going to ride a bike, sing in the school play, or learn to like broccoli. As you grew older you began to be more conscious of your aims in life. Maybe you saw yourself as a fire-fighter in the making, or possibly your aims were less defined, such as using your love of technology to make a living. The point is that you've always had goals one way or another, so you may as well make sure that they're the right ones. Given they're so fundamental, let's take a closer look at targets and goals – they are one and the same – and how you can use them to benefit your career.

HOW AMBITIOUS ARE YOU?

This was a question I was asked recently, and it gave me pause for thought. Ambition doesn't have to relate only to your job but also to how you can be the best possible version of yourself, whatever your ability. Do you want to earn a particular salary, achieve something for your family, or position yourself at a certain level in an organisation? What's important to you? You might not think of yourself as an ambitious person, but that doesn't mean you can't have progressive aims for your family or children, for instance. Or you might just want to be the best coder, cyclist or nurse you can be.

It's important to consider this because so often I see people set their sights lower than they need to. The fact is that we're all capable of much more than we think. Richard Branson often says that if someone offers you an amazing opportunity and you're not sure if you can manage it, just agree to it and learn how to do it afterwards. I would agree with him, and have long been of the view that if you say 'yes' often enough you'll soon be having an adventure. This is part of having a growth mindset, which is all about having a go without worrying too much about not succeeding – I encourage you to think like this, because you'll be amazed at the difference it can make.

I spoke with some super bright sixth-form students not long ago, and a couple of them said to me, 'I'm not going to try for Oxford or Cambridge.' I told them that was fine if they genuinely didn't want it for themselves, but not if it was because a fear of failure was stopping them. 'If someone were to hand an Oxbridge place to you right now with no strings attached,' I asked them, 'would you take it? If the answer's "yes", then why not give it a go? After all, what's the worst that can happen? You might not get in, but who cares?'

This is a great technique to use when you're feeling unsure about what's stopping you from aiming at a target that excites you, because it cuts across the excuses we give ourselves. When you're not worrying about *how* you're going to achieve something or *whether* you'll achieve it, but only *if* you would want it if it landed in your lap, you can focus on what you truly desire. This is the goal that's most meaningful to you, which is the best type there is. If you don't feel a little thrill when you think about it, you won't be prepared to go through the twists and turns you'll have to navigate before you reach it.

Talking of twists and turns, feeling excited about your end goal isn't the same as feeling good about every step of the road towards achieving it. If you limit yourself to what makes you happy right now, you'll be unlikely to reach the place you dreamed of at the beginning. When one of my sons started at university he found it hard to focus. I wanted to encourage him to try harder but when we spoke on the phone he said, 'Dad, I'm just trying to have a good time.' I wasn't impressed. 'Come on, you can do better than that,' I replied. 'That's not much of a goal, having a good time. It's fine to relax every now and then, but your degree won't happen on its own. You need to work as well.'

The great thing is when you have a target that lights you up, you'll gain energy you never thought you had and this will see you through the inevitable rough patches. On the other hand, if your goal is too safe or unimaginative you'll be unlikely to feel fired up about it.

HOW TO PICK YOUR TARGET

The word 'pick' is key here because a goal or target is something you should actively decide to have. The first aspect of this is to acknowledge that it's a good idea to have multiple goals, because just one would be limiting. They will ultimately create your purpose, and you want that to be as impactful as possible. As my father Alec Reed likes to say, 'None of us knows the length of our life but we can determine its width.'

You can also have goals which are either concrete or abstract. A concrete goal is something you can visualise or appreciate through your senses, such as buying a new house or working in a particular company. These are sometimes easier to set because it's obvious whether or not you've achieved them, but they can also be a trap. If your aims are to make a million pounds by the time you're thirty, climb Mount Everest, and buy a Lamborghini, that sounds exciting and if you truly want these things then good luck. But how about focusing on more abstract targets? These could include connecting people to one another, helping others to progress in their lives, strengthening your own character, or spending time supporting someone to fulfil their potential.

When I was interviewed on a radio show to talk about one of my books, I met an interesting fellow guest. She was a ninety-year-old woman who had been invited on the show to discuss the concept of kindness. Now in the tenth decade of her life she had concluded that kindness was the most important human attribute, and she spoke powerfully about its enduring impact. Little acts of kindness it seems, are long remembered. She made me realise that to develop kindness is not only a wonderful aim in its own right, but also draws people to you because it's such a valuable attribute to have. This will in turn help you to achieve all sorts of goals. When you aim at something that has a broader purpose than material gain you will feel good about it automatically, whereas if you're only seeking the next buzz, your enthusiasm will eventually fizzle out.

The best goals are the ones for which a deeper meaning is integral to them because that gives you the energy to keep pursuing them. I'm not saying there's anything wrong with concrete goals and I'm sure you already have some, but I encourage you to look wider than that. As my new friend in the green room said, 'If you can be anything, be kind.'

The steps to take

There are plenty of factors to take into account when you choose your targets, so let's break this down into a simple process.

First, consider your passions, values and purpose. It's important that your goals spring from these personal drivers because this way they're *your* targets, not ones that anyone else could have imposed upon you. You'll own them.

With these in mind, close your eyes and think about where you'd like to be in ten or twenty years' time. What do you want to have achieved by then? What do you want to be doing? Who do you want to be with? Where would you like to be headed? You don't have to tell anyone about it if you don't want to – it's your dream, your way. Then work back from that, because the targets you set yourself now should help you to get there. When you set off on a journey it begins, as Lao Tzu said, with a single step, and each subsequent step should bring you closer to your destination. Also, the road doesn't have to be straight; as I mentioned before, it's the winding ones that lead us to the most interesting places.

If you're in your twenties this is a really fun exercise, even if it's hard to think that far ahead. If you're older you might find yourself feeling a greater sense of urgency about reaching your targets because there's less time to do it in, especially where your career is concerned. Either way I hope you find it a motivating process.

I'd like you to choose three targets, one for each of the following: your **career**, your **family** (or close friends) and your **wider community**. These three have an important relationship for the following reasons. The first is that progressing your career isn't just about applying for jobs, it's about broadening your horizons by having conversations with as many people as possible. The second is that we're all connected to other people in complex ways, and what we strive for never occurs in a vacuum. If you're a parent, your goals could be inspiring for your children, and if you're not, you could have an impact on your colleagues and other people around you. It's certainly a good idea to take them into consideration when you're setting your goals.

For me, a major career goal is to build a digital employment platform and to extend REED's reach. A family goal is to help one of my children go through the transition from education into work as best I can. And a community goal is to grow the coding course in London I described earlier, so that we can help more young people develop their skills. You can see that the first goal is a long-term one but the second two are shorter term – that's fine, as when one goal is reached I'll replace it with another one.

Once you have your goals, visualise them. How you do this is your decision, but here are some suggestions. You could create a vision board by cutting photos out of newspapers and magazines and sticking them onto a piece of cardboard. The images should represent your goals and what they mean to you, together with the positive feelings and knock-on benefits you'll receive when you've attained them. For instance, if you're wanting to leave your admin job to train as a teacher within the next couple of years, you could put a photo of a teacher who was important to you or of your children heading off to their first day of school on there. One of my colleagues in Cardiff has a framed photograph of a beach in Barbados placed firmly on his desk in front of his two computer screens. That, he tells me, is where he's headed for Christmas.

Another option is to simply sit down, close your eyes and imagine your outcome. Picture yourself enrolling in teacher training college and then going up to collect your qualification. Allow yourself to feel the emotion as you do this. You can even carry this forward to envisioning your first day in your new job. What's it like to go through the doors of the school for the first time? How do the children behave towards you? And how does it feel to meet your colleagues on that day? Immerse yourself in the process of envisioning your goal.

Once you're enthused about achieving your target, you can start thinking about how you're going to reach that first step. This can lead you in unexpected directions, which can be half the fun. I remember when I turned forty I had a young family and was working long hours in my business, and my wife Nicola told me she was going to the gym. I realised that I hadn't been for a while and asked if I could go with her. We ran on the treadmill side by side and I was mortified to see that she was flying along while I was gasping for breath. 'This is terrible,' I thought. 'How has it come to this?' The experience started me thinking about how I could become fitter. I quickly decided running on its own would be too boring, so I should enter a race. This led to me completing a half marathon and several more, and finally the full-length marathons in Paris, London and New York. In fact, this target is a good example of how they can have an impact (both positive and negative) on those around you. Every Saturday I'd embark on a three- or four-hour training run to build my stamina, which with several small children at home was not particularly popular with Nicola.

AFTER THE TARGET

So you have your goals and you're clear on the steps you need to achieve them, or at least the first few. But how do you know if you've set the right ones? One clue to having chosen the wrong ones is if you consistently fail to achieve them. I once decided I wanted to learn the guitar, so I took lessons and practised diligently, but found it difficult and unrewarding. Eventually I worked out that I'd be better off spending my time on something more within my abilities. My alternative was singing lessons (much to my family's dismay). It's fine to abandon a goal, or to change it to something less challenging if you feel it's not working out. If the time and effort it takes is disproportionate to what you'd achieve from it then let it go. It's the same with your job or a course you're studying – if you've picked the wrong one, just move on.

The truth is that you'll only know if a target is the right one by going for it. If it's correct you'll feel happy with it, and if not you won't. For instance, if my attempts at learning the guitar had resulted in me feeling more relaxed after work, I might have carried on with it. When you abandon a goal, do please replace it with another one. It would be a shame to decide you're not up to something and then decide not to have any more ambitions as a result. You make the goals; they don't make you.

Of course, if your target is quantifiable, such as raising a certain amount of money for a charity or achieving a promotion, it's easy to know if you've reached it. In my case, I'll ask myself whether I've managed to help my children find work they enjoy, and if our business website has reached enough new users. That's the benefit of having a mix of concrete and abstract targets.

One thing to beware of is what's sometimes called the 'bereavement of achievement'. This is when you reach a target that was especially important to you, or that took an enormous amount of effort to accomplish, and then feel a bit lost and empty for a while afterwards. The best way to deal with this is to move straight on to a new one, otherwise you can become too attached to your previous goal. After all, the purpose of it was to help you reach a place you would otherwise never have arrived at – there's no intrinsic value in the goal itself.

As you grow older the nature of your ambitions will change. These days I gain more satisfaction from trying to do things that have a positive effect on people than I do from activities that are all about me. It's less 'Can I reach the top of this mountain?' and more 'Can I forge a message in my book that might help someone to do something great?'

If, having considered this, you're still not sure whether goal-setting is worthwhile, ask yourself to what extent you've ended up where you are now because of the choices you've made along the way. I'm sure you'll realise how powerful it is to have targets that you actively decide to go for rather than to just to be swept along by life, because they give you the direction and energy to achieve what you really want. Whatever this is will be completely personal to you and is closely bound up with what makes you the best version of yourself – in other words, what turns out to be your life's work.

WHAT WE COVERED

- Goals shape your life, so it's worth making sure that you have positive ones.
- When you set yourself a target, make it a challenging one and you'll achieve more than you think.

- To choose your targets start with your values, passions and purpose.
- Then visualise where you want to end up and work out the steps to travelling there.
- Once you've achieved what you want, start the next journey!

AND JUST ASKING . . .

- Which three goals will you now set yourself?
- How will you measure whether you've achieved them?

CHAPTER 7

Think in Days and Decades

One of the first things I do every morning is to take out my phone and check my company cash flow. Cash is the oxygen of any business, and just as we cannot live without air for more than three minutes, a company that runs out of cash will go under within days. I have to be sure that we're bringing in the revenue we need to pay our staff and suppliers, which means keeping a constant eye on our day-to-day performance.

However, although my focus is often on how the business is doing that day, I also have a long-term plan for growing it into the future. At the moment this consists of creating the next generation of flexible work online by building new digital employment services, a process that may take three to five years, or more, to deliver results. I'm travelling along two time horizons: the short-term one that focuses on delighting our customers today so that we can survive and fund our growth, and the extended one that ensures the organisation is future-proof.

You may be wondering what's happened to the period in the middle, between now and a few years' time. The answer is that it doesn't really exist for me. Ask me what my holiday dates are for next year, for instance, and I wouldn't be able to tell you because my work exists either in the immediacy of today or in the imagined future. These timelines are what drive me.

This approach to life can be hard to get your head around because it can feel like you're running on two tracks at the same time – the 100-metre and the marathon. But it's a mindset that many entrepreneurs adopt. In my experience, the most successful ones are able to concentrate on the immediate present and at the same time dare to imagine the unforeseeable future. In their 'day' view they're alert to opportunities that arise before them, and in their 'decade' view they're inspired by where they want to be many years from now.

You may not necessarily see yourself as an entrepreneur, but you're still managing the trajectory of your own career. It's like you're imagining and inventing it for yourself, just as a business owner takes responsibility for creating their product or service. And similarly to that entrepreneur, when you're at work you should be completely absorbed in figuring out how you're going to make a difference right now *as well as* having a grand vision of where you want to be in ten years' time. Because it's only when you have that powerful combination running inside your head that you can make the little improvements that accumulate into significant ones *and* take decisions that move you up to a whole new level. Weirdly the space in the middle isn't too important – it will be there when it comes, but it's not essential to think about right now.

'The harder I practise, the luckier I get,' is a quote often attributed to star golfer Gary Player. This sums up the days and decades approach perfectly, because feeling fulfilled in your work comes from a combination of doing a brilliant job right now and having a plan for the future. Depending on your age and scope, ask yourself: 'Where do I want to be when I'm thirty, forty, fifty or beyond?' This chapter will help you to understand the timing landscape of your career, so that you can have the job you want now without losing momentum for the 'you' you want to be in the future.

THE SEVEN AGES OF MAN

'All the world's a stage, and all the men and women merely players,' wrote William Shakespeare in *As You Like It*. He went on to detail how each person's life is made up of seven ages, from the baby 'mewling and puking in the nurse's arms', to childhood, young adulthood, middle age, old age, and finally to 'second childishness and mere oblivion'. Assuming that we work from when we leave education to when we retire at around the age of seventy (for that's when it will be for many of us), most of us can expect to have around fifty years of active, functioning adult life. How should you use yours? What's the best way of thinking about who you want to be, and what you want to contribute, in the different phases of your life?

From a career perspective I like to break the years into three groups of ages: eighteen to thirty, thirty to fifty, and fifty to seventy. These are approximate, of course, but they make thinking about the future easier than imagining the rest of your life in one go. A career that might have suited you at the age of twenty-five might not exist any more by the time you're fifty, or there may be a transformation in your organisation or industry that propels you into a different area. What's more, many workplaces will transform themselves during the time you can expect to be at them. Think of the job titles that are commonplace now but that didn't exist a few years ago:

- App developer
- Barista
- Cloud computing specialist
- Social media manager
- Uber driver
- UX designer
- Vlogger
- Zumba instructor

The list goes on. Being open and alive to new opportunities as you grow older is vital, as is being patient. There's a wise saying that I love: 'It takes twenty years to create an overnight success.' When you look at the top athletes of today, they've been training since they were kids. It's rare to achieve a breakthrough without years of effort. It also takes time to carve out a fulfilling career, so it's worth pacing yourself. With that in mind, let's look at the three career stages in turn, so you can see how to make the most of each one.

EIGHTEEN TO THIRTY

It's a paradox that the early years of your career are probably the most daunting and, at the same time, the most exciting. There you are, standing on the threshold of your adult life, and it feels like it's going to last for ever. It's a wonderful (and essential) period to learn, travel and experiment. Now is the time to discover what floats your boat: what you really want to do, where you'd like to live and who you'd like to share your life with. Your goal should be to learn as much as you can and to develop yourself into a broader, deeper and more accomplished person by the time you're thirty. This might involve further training and education, varying the jobs you do, or taking up new hobbies and activities.

In the process you're bound to make mistakes, and I'd say that if you don't look back on this period with some element of rueful regret you probably haven't lived it to the full. Often I come across young people who are worried about their future. 'I messed up my studies,' they say. 'Well, how old are you?' I ask. 'I'm nineteen,' is the reply. Or, 'This is my third job and I'm still not happy. I'm twenty-seven now – when will I find the kind of work I love?' To this I say, 'You have another fifty years to go, so don't worry about the odd wrong turn at this stage. You're doing exactly what you're meant to be doing – trying things out.'

In my twenties I did some wildly different things, which I'm glad about because it was before I married and had children so I had the freedom to experiment. One of my richest learning experiences was going to Afghanistan as an aid worker. I'd raised money for a charity there while at home, and found myself fascinated by the country so I decided to help out on the ground. I'm not sure what I expected, but after a couple of weeks working in intense heat while in a refugee camp, I travelled further afield and found myself in a desolate valley that had been attacked by the Russians and was in the midst of a malaria epidemic. It was a harrowing experience, with families surviving in bombed-out houses nursing their sick children and relatives. One afternoon I was startled by the terrifying sound of explosives which were part of an attack that turned into a full-blown air raid.

As you can see, I lived to tell the tale, but the experience has stayed with me for life. Although I didn't realise it at the time, living in such tough conditions and being in constant danger made me more resilient – if I could survive that, surely problems at work would pale into insignificance. I wouldn't necessarily recommend that you do something similar, but it was certainly formative for me!

Three questions to ask yourself in your twenties

- 'What excites me right now?'
- 'Where do I want to be in ten years' time, and what experience and knowledge will help me to get there?'
- 'What kind of person do I want to be when I'm older?'

Three adventures to have in your twenties

- Try to work for someone you can learn from, however lowly the job may be.
- See if you can study or work abroad, or at least in another part of the country – make sure it's well away from home.

- Find a role that you love, even if it's not in the industry you'd planned for yourself.

THIRTY TO FIFTY

This can be a wonderful period of your career because you're experienced enough to feel competent and secure in what you do, but you also have the energy and vision to achieve a huge amount more. You're riding the crest of the wave that's been building since you left education. With any luck you've discovered what it is you want to achieve with your life, and even if you haven't it's not too late (although you need to get your skates on). You should also have the answers to the questions you asked yourself above, in your twenties. You might decide to revisit them and change course, and that's fine, but at least you have something solid to base your plans on.

This should be your peak delivery period, because you know what you're doing and you have the energy and enthusiasm to do a great job. Your expectations of yourself should be high – you can be at the top of your game if you want, not necessarily in terms of how much money you earn but in how fulfilled you are by your work and how well you perform it. You're probably earning more than you did in your twenties, which is no bad thing if you have a family and mortgage to manage. There are also likely to be multiple demands on your time, as you juggle increased responsibility at work with caring responsibilities at home, in which case you'll be glad you had some carefree fun when you had the chance.

Despite these energising aspects, it's a time when you might start to question the wisdom of being where you are now. This is common and is often dubbed a 'mid-life crisis'. There doesn't have to be anything crisis-ridden about it, however. You'll be working for another twenty or thirty years, so why not take stock? If you started in business and think that you'd prefer to move into education or the creative sector, for instance, you'd have a huge amount to offer. Your pre-existing experience and skills will give your CV an added dimension when it comes to exploring these new worlds.

Three questions to ask yourself in your thirties to fifties

- 'Is this what I want to carry on doing for the second half of my life?'
- 'Do I have a dream that's been left unfulfilled?'
- 'What have I proved to be good at? What makes me special?'

Three explorations to make in your thirties to fifties

- Carry out a skills and experience audit by listing the main attributes you can bring to any organisation.
- Widen your experience by seeking a role in a new industry or sector.

- Go for that promotion – you're at the ideal time to win it.

FIFTY TO SEVENTY

The later stages of your career are the ideal period to take stock of the experience and skills that you've accumulated. It's also a time when you have added perspective on your work, which is a quality that only the years can give. You might start to wonder about the legacy you'll leave. When you were in your twenties you were more self-oriented, and rightly so, but now your thinking might be more to do with the context you live in – whether that be your family, colleagues or community. Life now is as much about what you can contribute and give back as it is about what you can gain for yourself. This can take many forms – you might be a mentor to a younger person, or donate your time and money in other ways. You're starting to think about your work in a broader sense, and in fact that's why I'm writing this book now, in the hope that my experience might be helpful in some way to other people.

If you're driven in your career, the time period from fifty to seventy can also be when you end up running things. It could be a company, a school, a theatre outfit – whatever excites you. If you've excelled in your work and are still ambitious, you can take the reins and fulfil your career destiny. It's now or never.

Apart from anything else, it's necessary to have a positive approach to work during these years. As I write, the official state pension age in the UK is sixty-five (due to rise to sixty-seven in the near future), and retirement isn't compulsory like it used to be. This means that you're going to work into your late sixties at the very least, and maybe into your seventies, which is great news if you love your job. Especially now that most work isn't physically taxing, you have the opportunity to extend your working life and be an incredible contributor at the same time.

The most helpful way you can support yourself is to maintain your health and keep your energy levels high. Taking regular exercise and looking after your diet is even more important than when you were younger – if you're anything like me, I know that I could stay out all night every weekend when I was twenty but I'm not interested in doing that now. Especially if you're in any position of authority, you must look after your body, because who wants a tired, old leader?

Of course, not everyone wants to work at full tilt until they're in their seventies. You might prefer to travel, go part-time or do voluntary work instead. These options can be rewarding, and you've earned the right to be selective about where you expend your energies. On the other hand, like an accountant who once worked for me, you might yearn to retire to an allotment. On his first day in the job he told me that he planned to retire in eight years' time to do gardening, and true to his promise, he did. He was an excellent accountant and his choice was fine with me, but I found it curious that he was spending his career in a role that didn't fulfil him. If he wanted to garden, he could have become a gardener or set up his own horticultural business.

Which brings me to my final point about this rich and

rewarding time of your career. If you're in your fifties and are unhappy with your job, you still have another twenty years to find and do something else. Please don't go into retirement regretting that you didn't take action sooner – fifty is a perfectly good age to start a second career. Some people say companies are ageist and don't want to give older people a chance, but in my experience they're more energist than ageist. What they want are individuals with commitment, presence and application, rather than those who are the 'right' age. You can find practical advice on how to create a winning CV for a career shift in my book *The 7 Second CV* – there's a section in it with tactics and examples to suit your particular needs.

As for myself, as long as my health remains good, I hope to stay working until I'm at least seventy-five and plan to be fully engaged and happily contributing to the business. I might reduce my hours or delegate more than I do now, but I certainly don't think of sixty or seventy as being past it. If you want to hang up your boots I hope you have a long and happy retirement, but if you want to continue developing your career there are growing opportunities to do that.

Three questions to ask yourself in your fifties to seventies

- 'Is this job or career the one that I still want?'
- 'What kind of legacy would I like to leave?'
- 'How can I best use the skills and experience that I've accumulated?'

Three challenges to give yourself in your fifties to seventies

- Find someone, or some people, to mentor through the early stages of their career.
- If you're not happy with where you are now, do something about it this year.
- Ask yourself if you have relevant experience to contribute to your community or colleagues, and find a way to share it.

THE VALUE OF THE MOMENT

Not long ago, a friend of mine who's in a band invited me to the recording of his new live album in a London music venue. As I entered the tiny theatre and threaded my way between the tables to the front of the stage, I felt a sense of anticipation as I realised how close I'd be to the main event. Drink in hand, I eagerly anticipated the evening of ringside entertainment to come.

First up was a solo singer who was part of the recording, followed by another, and they were both excellent. After them came the soul star Beverley Knight. As she walked onto the stage I could see she was in total focus. Smiling at the audience, she took her place at the mic and closed her eyes in preparation. After a deep breath she threw back her head, opened her mouth, and released a stream of the most beautiful, powerful notes I'd heard in a long time. I was spellbound. Here was a woman who was utterly absorbed by her craft, and because I was standing so close to her could I witness the intensity of it. Her energy was high, she knew her moves and her notes to perfection, and the result was outstanding. I'm sure that when she finished and left the stage she put her feet up and checked her phone just like anyone else, but for the time she was doing that job she was doing nothing (and I mean nothing) else but that.

This is what I mean by giving everything to the present moment. What do you give to your job in energy, preparation and care each and every day? Because when you focus on what you're doing right here and right now, your performance will be the best that it can be. This is another trait that I've seen in successful entrepreneurs – they throw themselves into the 'now' and wring every last drop of inspiration and productivity from it. It's something that I try to do as well. For instance, if someone walks into my office, my first thought is how to make them feel welcome so that they feel willing and able to give their best. I don't think, 'I've got to make four phone calls before lunch, how on earth am I going to find time for this person too?'

Being in the moment is a mindset and it's the opposite of multitasking. Beverley Knight was certainly not multitasking when she gave that performance; she was completely focused on the job in hand. If you want to be a top performer this is how you need to approach your work. Having a long-term drive is part of success, but being super-present is the other half of the equation. This is where thinking in days and decades comes into its own.

WHAT WE COVERED

- Being focused on the day today, and also on what you want to achieve in ten years' time, is the key to being the successful creator of your career.
- From eighteen to thirty your focus is on trying different things, travelling and learning.
- From thirty to fifty your focus is on making the most of your experience and moving yourself up to the next level.
- From fifty to seventy your focus is on planning your legacy and using this last opportunity to fulfil your potential.
- It's just as important to live in the present moment as it is to plan for the years ahead.

AND JUST ASKING . . .

- If you could volunteer for something outside of work, what would it be?
- What other jobs can you think of that didn't exist five years ago?

CHAPTER 8

Be Powerful, Be Prepared

On one of my office walls hangs a framed photo that I find particularly inspiring. It shows a man bundled into a waterproof jacket, grinning through his beard and wreathed in climbing ropes slung around his body. A thin layer of frost covers the ropes, and in his hands he holds a set of walking poles. Behind him, just visible through a raging blizzard, rear the upper levels of a snow-covered mountain. This man is my friend Stefan Gatt, who was the first person in the world to climb Mount Everest without oxygen and then to snowboard down from the top (crazy, I know). It was a phenomenal achievement, but it wasn't luck that gave him his success. It was meticulous preparation.

Taking the time to prepare for a dangerous mountaineering expedition seems like a pretty obvious thing to do, but you'd be surprised at how many people skimp on it. I've done a fair bit of mountain-climbing myself and whenever I hear awful stories of adventurers dying in the snow, too often it turns out to be because they didn't have the right kit or check the weather conditions properly.

A few hours of planning could have made the difference between life and death.

You may be wondering what this has to do with your career, and it's this: being prepared can make or break its success. That's why I keep the picture of Stefan close by, because it reminds me of the importance of being ready for all eventualities. Preparation gives you power and confidence, and is relevant for every area of work. In my experience the people with well-considered arguments, ideas they've tested out and a professional level of presentation are far more impressive than those who are always trying to wing it. Preparation also has integrity, because it enables you to be respectful of other people's time and attention.

There are many other benefits to being prepared. You're able to start new initiatives easily because everything is in place from the beginning. You're likely to spot potential pitfalls so you can come up with solutions in advance. And by thinking up front, you may identify strengths and weaknesses in your course of action so that you can work out what to do about them ahead of time. Put focus, energy and time into being strong, smart and prepared. Stefan didn't just throw a few belongings together and check the weather report before he set off on his adventure, he thoroughly readied himself in both mind and body.

Of course, being in a *constant* state of readiness is impossible, but you can prioritise the most important occasions. We'll cover them here and reveal a secret weapon for your career – when you keep abreast of changes appearing over the horizon, you're unlikely to ever be caught on the hop again. Being prepared is not glamorous or sexy, but my goodness it's powerful.

HOW TO BE A PREPARATION NINJA

I use the word 'ninja' with a smile, because I'm the first to admit that the ability to plan with precision isn't my top trait. I envy those who do it with ease (I can't count how many birthdays I've forgotten). I've had to *learn* to become better at it, and much of that process has been through trial and error. Anyone can upgrade their organisation skills – you just have to decide to do it. All it takes is a bit of time and effort.

It's easy to underestimate the extent to which many small tasks done well can enhance your work performance. Set yourself the goal of always being well prepared, and be disciplined about it. Planning doesn't have to take long, and half the battle is remembering to factor it in – just give yourself enough time. If you tend to forget about planning, schedule a slot in your calendar a few days before an important interview or meeting. And if you're naturally good at it, please be sure to value this skill and make sure you emphasise it in job interviews. You'll find that the more you use it in your career, the more sought-after you'll be.

I'm going to give you some tips on preparing for what I see as the three main leverage moments that you'll come across in most jobs: interviews, presentations and meeting people for the first time. These are usually the times when you're most able to have an impact on someone, and with some planning you can make sure you turn them to your advantage.

PREPPING FOR INTERVIEWS

Job interviews are an important time to be prepared. In fact, a lack of preparation is the main reason that applicants are rejected. How much time does this take? Not long – you only need to read up on some interview techniques and think about how you'll answer the most likely questions. My book about how to do this, *Why You? 101 Interview Questions You'll Never Fear Again*, has helped thousands of candidates to perform more confidently and land the job of their dreams. Quite simply, the people who prepare for interviews are the ones who are offered the jobs.

It starts with being curious. It's amazing what you can discover online about the company you're applying to and the people who will be interviewing you. For a start, it means that you can dodge a bullet if the organisation isn't financially sound. If you log on to the Companies House website you can search for their company accounts. I love doing this as it satisfies my nosy nature, and when people leave our business for pastures new I often look up the financial situation of their new organisation. If the business is making a loss, has no cash and is riddled with debt, they shouldn't be expecting promotions and pay rises. If they had done their due diligence they could have worked this out for themselves ahead of time, rather than possibly regretting their decision later.

You can also search online for the senior people in the organisation you're applying to, using Companies House and LinkedIn. Glassdoor is a place where you can find honest employee reviews, and if you know anyone who's been a customer of the firm, or who's worked there, even better. Given that you may be thinking about spending at least three years of your life in that new place, why wouldn't you do your homework first? A word of warning, however. Your cyber search might leave you super well informed about the personal life and preferences of your interviewer. But you don't want to spook them by dropping in that you spotted them on the final of *The Apprentice*, and that you know they have six kids, a wife called Nicola and a tortoise called John Terry . . . just saying!

Once you're clear on the organisation and people side of things, it's time to prepare your interview answers. Naturally you can't predict every question that you'll be asked, but there are some obvious ones that there's no excuse for ignoring. I call them the 'Fateful Fifteen', and my research has shown that these fifteen questions do in fact form the basis of all job interviews:

- 'Tell me about yourself.'
- 'Why are you applying?'
- 'What are your greatest strengths?'
- 'What are your greatest weaknesses?'
- 'What will your skills and ideas bring to this company?'
- 'What's your preferred management style?'
- 'Where do you see yourself in five years' time?'
- 'How would you approach this job?'
- 'What have you achieved elsewhere?'
- 'What did you like and dislike about your last job?'
- 'Tell me about a time you worked in a team.'
- 'What do your colleagues say about you?'
- 'How do you deal with stress and failure?'

- 'How much money do you want?'
- 'Show me your creativity.'

If you do nothing else, work out what you'd say to each of these key lines of interrogation and you won't go far wrong. You'll be streets ahead of most of the other candidates, many of whom won't have made it past number four. Even better, you'll feel more relaxed and confident, which will send out signals that you'd be a competent and happy person to have around.

PREPPING FOR PRESENTATIONS

I've yet to meet anyone who loves preparing a presentation, but giving a talk is definitely one of those occasions when you can't wing it and expect to make it a success. Yes, there are rare individuals who seem to be able to speak at a moment's notice, carrying the audience with them as lightly as a feather, but if you're like most people you probably need to plan in advance.

Actually, it's surprising how often gifted presenters aren't as spontaneous as they first seem. A friend of mine once saw Boris Johnson arrive at an event to give a talk, and watched as he scribbled some notes while he was waiting. Boris then strode onto the stage and gave a brilliant speech which had everyone laughing – utter brilliance. A week later my friend happened to be at another event at which Boris was to speak, and watched him go through some rehearsals and deliver exactly the same talk. It still went down like a storm but it was planned, not spontaneous.

On a more painful note, I remember one fateful occasion on which I and my team were due to pitch for a website build for a prestigious external organisation based on the other side of London. We'd rehearsed thoroughly during the week before, and duly set off in good time in my family van along with our gear. As we approached the venue, the traffic slowly ground to a halt, but I wasn't too worried as we had an hour to spare. What I hadn't realised was that there was a student demonstration taking place around the corner, which resulted in total gridlock. I watched the minutes tick by with agonising slowness until we decided to abandon the van, pick up our projector, and run to the meeting on foot. Needless to say we arrived late and dripping with sweat, and the whole pitch was a disaster. It was so frustrating because we would have done a brilliant job on that website, and if I'd only thought to check the traffic before we left we'd have had a good chance of securing the business.

So what's the first thing that you should do when you're asked to present? Rather than fire up your laptop and start creating slides, think about what you want your main message to be. What's the key thing that you intend your audience to go away thinking and feeling? This is far more important than brainstorming a heap of points and details, many of which will go over everyone's heads. Presenting is definitely one of those occasions where less is more. I'm not going to give you a detailed rundown of how to plan a talk here, but there are heaps of books that explain how to do it. They should all guide you in how to make an impact, whether it be visually or verbally, how to keep your audience's attention, and how to ensure everyone goes away impressed with the clarity of what you've put across. One that I can recommend is *The Busy Person's Guide to Great Presenting* by Lee Warren.

Don't be like the giver of the second of two talks I sat through recently, both from tech companies who were bidding to develop our database. The first outfit brought ideas, insights and suggestions that were relevant for our needs, and their presentation was also well rehearsed. The second group should by rights have been better prepared as it had carried out more work for us over the years, but it was a shambles. The lead presenter even had his shirt hanging out and his jumper halfway up his stomach (not a good look). If this was his judgement on how to present to me, what would it have been like for anything else he planned to do? I wasn't motivated to get my chequebook out.

When you present in a prepared way you know that what you have to say is interesting and good, and this gives you confidence when you stand up to communicate it. You will come across as poised and powerful.

PREPPING FOR IMPORTANT MEETINGS

There are many reasons why a meeting might be important. There's the obvious example – the gathering where you're wanting to impress key people, or to make an impact with a significant message – but it could also be your first day in a new job, or an introduction to the chief executive. In all of these scenarios, the better you've planned ahead of time, the more confidently you'll handle them.

Taking the first example to start with – a meeting where you want to make a great impression – knowing your stuff is essential. Your first task is to understand the purpose of the session and why you're there. Is it to update people, debate an issue or guide everyone towards a specific decision? Knowing what you want to achieve will make it more likely that you'll come away with the buy-in that you need.

Next, create a list of the people who will be there and what you can say to win over each of them. It might be that you're wanting to gain approval for a new project, and that different individuals will have their own vested interests. Or you could feel strongly that a particular course of action is the best way to solve a company problem, and want to influence the decision. What examples and facts can you present that will bring the participants to your side?

You can see from this how essential it is to be prepared. Apart from anything else, you'll avoid feeling embarrassed if you're challenged on a point and can't answer it. When I ask someone a question in a meeting, I expect them to know the answer. If you've done your homework it shows.

There are other occasions on which you might want to impress people. Being introduced to someone important for the first time is a key one, and by 'important' I mean all sorts of things. It could be that the individual is at a senior level in your organisation, or maybe they're a new colleague or client. The more you can find out about them beforehand the better, as being able to come up with a relevant fact or opinion about them is impressive. In fact, powerful business people often ask their assistants to brief them on those they're due to meet so that they can do just that – 'Ah, Mrs Smith, how lovely to see you again. And how are the twins?' You can be your own PA and do this for yourself.

PREPPING FOR THE UNEXPECTED

So often, career success comes down to a few key moments, and you never know when they're going to come. The chance encounter with someone who recommends you for a job. A surprise promotion. Or, less positively, a redundancy or relocation that you hadn't predicted was on the cards. You can't always foresee these events but you can be defined by how you react to them, and much of that comes down to preparation. As the saying goes, 'Success is where preparation and opportunity meet.' If you've done your spadework beforehand you'll be in a strong position to take advantage of whatever life throws at you.

It's possible to go through your career with blinkers on, so when shifts in your industry or organisation arise they can come as a shock. But was it realistic to think that things were going to stay the same for ever? You only have to look in the mirror every day to see that change is inevitable; in fact, the least likely scenario is that the world of work will stay constant. Thinking about what you would do if your role were to be no more, or if you had to move to a different part of the country due to factors outside your control, helps you to deal with it if it happens. A major element of this is to stay connected and keep 'going to parties'. That way you'll be likely to intercept any rumours afoot, and even if you don't pick up on anything, you'll still be refreshing your relationships with your contacts – invaluable if you need to look for another job.

On a day-to-day level there's the unexpected event at work or home that we've all experienced – the kind when your day is turned upside down because the finance director has pulled the budget on your project, or your boiler breaks down and you have to wait at home for a plumber. The more organised you are, the less difficult you'll find this to cope with. A quick check of your to-do list for the day and you're ready to decide what to do or ditch.

A lesson that it took me a while to learn was that if a crisis explodes you need to drop what you're doing and head straight to wherever you need to be, and fast. Just switch your plans. When one of my sons was little I was in an important board meeting and a call came to tell me that he'd hit his head at school and was in hospital. I rushed straight there, where I saw him lying pale on the bed with his eyes closed. The nurse squeezed his cheek, only to be greeted with a fantastic grin – my boy had nothing wrong with him after all. Sometimes a crisis isn't a crisis, but you won't know until you've responded!

The truth is that there are few incidents which can't be dealt with most effectively when you're prepared, either by considering how you'd react or by planning what can be controlled so that you have bandwidth to cope with what can't. If you have savings to pay for your boiler repair, for instance, life is so much easier than if you've blown them on weekend breaks. Spontaneity is exciting but is seldom sufficient. After all, when Oscar Wilde strode through New York customs control and quipped, 'I have nothing to declare except my genius,' he knew he was going to be there ahead of time. In his case, preparation was part of what sealed his reputation as a wit and literary genius.

WHAT WE COVERED

- Being prepared gives you power, because you can take advantage of positive situations and make the best of negative ones.
- The most common situations in which it's important to be well prepared are job interviews, presentations and meetings of various kinds.
- When you have a job interview, take the time to research the organisation and think about the answers you would give to questions beforehand.
- When you make a presentation, rehearsing your message is essential for winning over your audience.
- When you're being introduced to someone for the first time, or in an important meeting, knowing your objectives and something about the other person enables you to come across as knowledgeable and credible.

AND JUST ASKING . . .

- Can you think of a time when you were badly prepared and regretted it? What would you do differently next time?
- What's the next opportunity you can prepare for?

CHAPTER 9

Showcase Your Work Ethic

If you look up the meaning of the phrase 'work ethic', you'll see it's defined as appreciating the value of hard work or of putting long hours into your job. However, I have a different take on it. What I mean by work ethic is the level of commitment and engagement you have with your endeavours, rather than the amount of time you spend doing them.

This is important because when you're 'all in' with your work, you raise yourself out of the mainstream. Which person is more likely to gain the respect of their colleagues and managers, and also be promoted? The individual who sees themself as a cog in the machine, mentally ticking boxes so that they can say they've completed their allotted tasks by the end of the day? Or the person who actively avoids working on autopilot and is always looking for ways to improve things for their organisation? If you're not too worried about progressing and doing well, and have other priorities, that's fine. But if you want to build a career that's more challenging and satisfying than that, your work ethic is key.

Of course, this doesn't mean that you won't also work

hard. If you look at the most successful entrepreneurs, for instance, they usually combine an all-encompassing dedication to their mission with long hours at the coalface. But when you enjoy what you do this doesn't feel onerous – on the contrary, it's energising to throw yourself into the challenge of succeeding in your role. It's possible to work *too* hard, or to give too much to your work, but this isn't something I frequently observe. I find that the other end of the spectrum, that of not giving enough, is much more common. This is why the people who do go the extra mile tend to be the most successful – they stand out by being fully present and engaged.

WHAT DOES A POSITIVE WORK ETHIC LOOK LIKE?

If you look around your workplace, you'll probably realise that there's a small number of people who stand out from the crowd. They seem energised, enthusiastic and purposeful, and if they're well managed they also have the quickest progressing careers. How do they do it? What makes them special? In my experience, there are three key characteristics of someone with a positive work ethic and anyone can develop them – you just have to know what they are.

Valuing customer care above everything else

At REED, our business strategy is to grow organically rather than by acquiring other businesses. There are only two ways we can do this: through giving excellent service to our customers, and through innovating. For this reason, the qualities I most value in people are a passion for service and the ability to come up with new ideas. This is a useful approach for you, too. Just like a business, you want to grow your career organically (after all, you can't acquire anyone else to do it for you), and also to develop as a person in your job. The best ways to do this are by always giving attentive service to your customers and being someone who never stops thinking about ways to improve. A job is a problem to be solved, so how can you do that better than anyone else?

Everyone has customers at work, whether they are internal or external. For instance, you could be in a finance team, in which case your internal customers are other people in your organisation, or you could be a sales person, in which case your customers are the people buying directly from you. It's how well you serve them that matters. What's more, it's possible to find value in all your tasks, even the ones that you don't enjoy or that seem trivial to you. Your work ethic is reflected in how fully you throw yourself into performing them well.

As for ideas, I love it when people come up with them because it shows that they're thinking more widely than the narrow requirements of their role. I've never come across a job description that specified the number of ideas a person is expected to have – now there's an idea in itself – but as I've always been taught, we should try to come up with an idea a day at least. They won't all be good ones or even necessarily come to fruition, but the few that do can make a huge difference to you and your company.

Constantly self-improving

I've always thought that mediocre people are the hardest to manage, because they sit between the poor performers (who I know what to do with) and the stars (who can be left to get on with it). It's the ones in the middle – usually the majority in any organisation – who are the hardest to shift into a positive work ethic.

This also applies to you as an individual. If you can move your day-to-day endeavours from strictly average to the top 10 per cent, you'll see the benefits of that in your career when you find yourself enjoying your work more and being promoted. Just asking yourself, 'Do I want to fly on autopilot or do I want to be a top gun?' can make all the difference.

Fostering quality relationships with colleagues

One element of your work ethic is how you interact with your team-mates. What's your first reaction when you see that someone needs a hand, or is having a difficult day? A helpful colleague is often the one who is most appreciated and respected. As you progress in your career you'll have increasing opportunities to make an impact on people, because you'll be developing the next generation of leaders, managers, specialists and other staff. Your approach to your work will be shown through them as much as it is through your own productivity – not only are you carrying out your 'day job', you're inspiring others too. This doesn't have to be just at work, either, it can be in your community or more widely within your profession.

THE LONG HOURS CULTURE

I hope by now you're clear that showcasing your work ethic isn't the same as working from dawn until dusk (even though it may sometimes involve it), it's about being fully committed to contributing to your organisation. However, it's worth examining the notion of what some people call the 'long hours culture', because the assumption that working well is equated with working 'long' is one that's become embedded in our business culture, incorrectly I'd argue.

I see constant long hours as the way work used to be done. Sending emails late at night, calling the office on holiday, and feeling that you can't leave before anyone else in case you look like a slacker – these can become unhealthy habits. For most people it isn't sustainable, and your work ethic will burn out over time if you overdo things. There's nothing wrong with setting some boundaries, especially now that our phones have blurred the distinction between work and family life. I'm sure that if there was an acute emergency at work you'd be happy to do whatever it takes, but most of the time urgent problems are rarely as important as they might seem at first. For instance, if our company website went down I'd see that as a class one crisis and would rush into the office to help sort it out, but even then I'd be aware that I'm not the one who has the expertise to fix it. I'd bring in my technical team and give them all the support I could.

One of the top professors at Harvard Business School is Clayton Christensen, who was once a high-level basketball player. He told me that when he was competing for Oxford University in his youth, his team reached the finals of a major tournament which was due to take place the following Sunday. A committed Christian, he turned down the opportunity to play because he'd made a promise to himself at the age of sixteen that he would always observe Sunday as a day of rest – a decision that, he said, was one of the most important he ever made because it eliminated a whole raft of subsequent ones. 'Just this once' – how often do we hear that? But he didn't have to think about it because he was crystal clear with himself on where he stood. In the same way, I take care to observe a day of rest and turn off my phone on Sundays – it's important that I and my colleagues have some space for ourselves.

Having said that, and this is where the topic becomes more nuanced, there's nothing wrong with working long hours if it's rewarding and productive for you, and if you're able to do so with passion and commitment. Speaking personally, I'm never completely clear about when work ends and home life begins because I work in a family company. I'm happy to read business papers on a Saturday because I find them interesting and enjoyable. And, like most business owners, I have an emotional stake in the company that goes further than it does for many people. I'm also not keen on the phrase 'work–life balance' because it suggests it's not possible to 'live' while you're at work. I prefer 'work–life integration', because work is a part of life – a vital one.

WHEN YOU ENJOY YOUR WORK IT'S EASY

You can see that working hard and working smart are not mutually exclusive as long as you're in a job in which you can be sustainably selfish. Putting in the effort doesn't feel like a burden then, it's just one of the ways that you express your work ethic. After all, your role is bigger than just you, because you're fulfilling a purpose. If you love what you do, why wouldn't you want to work hard at it?

There are many people whose work ethic I admire. Chief among them is my father, who is aged eighty-five and still going strong because he loves it. He sometimes calls REED his 'life's work', although that's usually when he's cautioning me about messing things up. Given he started the company when he was a young man and is still involved in it sixty years later, I'd say that he's showcasing a work ethic even though it's at a level that few of us will be able to match.

A way of helping yourself here is to keep a record of your achievements. This is not only motivating for you, but also helps you to talk about them when needed – the 'showcasing' element. I often advise our new recruitment consultants to jot down the names of all the people whom they've placed in jobs each month, because those are the ones whose lives they've positively impacted. They find this incredibly helpful and also to be a useful way of keeping themselves on track.

If you're finding it difficult to have a positive work ethic, take it as a hint that you might not be in the right job or in the right organisation. There's no harm in realising this, and it's something that most people go through at one time or another. I worked in advertising many years ago and enjoyed it for a while, but when it became repetitive I started to lose interest. As soon as I saw that my commitment was diminishing, I left and did something else.

You might also feel demotivated if you're trying to demonstrate a positive work ethic by coming up with ideas and making improvements, but nobody notices or you're blocked from implementing them. If this is due to your company's organisational culture, there's not a lot you can do about it apart from finding a new company or starting your own. But if it's due to the people you work with, remember that they're probably not going to be there for ever. You can decide to sit it out for now, or to leave and do something more enjoyable – either way, identify where the problem lies so that it doesn't eat away at your enthusiasm.

PROVING IT

Here's where we come to the showcasing of your work ethic. Some people find it hard to talk about their achievements – they think it sounds boastful and would rather fly under the radar than draw attention to themselves. I also think that women tend to find promoting their work more difficult than men. How often does a woman suggest an idea that a man gets the credit for, because he's quicker to claim it for his own than she is? However, if you care about what you do, people should be told about it.

In some jobs, such as sales, it's obvious how you rank amongst your peers in terms of results, but in others it's less apparent. Even in roles where success is less well defined, though, you'd be surprised how people notice when you're doing a good job. If you're determined, creative and enthusiastic, it will be remarked upon.

Of course, this doesn't mean that you want to be saying

to your boss, 'Ooh, look at me' every day. You'll have to find a way that works for your particular role and the culture of your organisation. When I think of the people in my company who have impressed me over the years, it's those who have made constructive suggestions who stand out. Constructive suggestions are different from complaints. Moaning about things without coming up with useful alternatives is frustrating for any leader. On the other hand, when people aren't afraid to point out a flaw to me and have ideas as to what to do instead, I invariably find it impressive. If you want to draw positive attention to yourself, why not identify a pain point in your company and come up with a fresh way of looking at it? Then your work ethic will be as plain as day.

WHEN THINGS GO WRONG

How you handle making a mistake is an integral part of showcasing your work ethic because it reveals a lot about your personal standards. If you're willing to admit you've messed up on something and make it clear that you want to put it right, it shows you have your organisation's best interests at heart. If you try to cover it up (or even worse, dress it up as a success or attempt to blame someone else), it's a sign that you're more concerned with protecting your reputation.

There's no shame in making a mistake – we all do it. In fact it's necessary, because if you're not regularly tripping up (hopefully in a small way) you're not doing or learning anything new. Recently I gave the go-ahead for a large project, and the person managing it came to me at the eleventh hour with the unwelcome news that it was going to cost £50,000 more than they had predicted. This was an issue on two levels. The first was that it showed the project wasn't being well managed, and the second was that his lateness gave us no time to come up with a possible solution. If you think something's going to go wrong, it's good to ask for help early on because at least you'll be showing you care about putting it right.

What if someone in your team makes a mistake or has some kind of crisis? Showing up and helping them is a great way of demonstrating your work ethic. This is something I've learned to become better at as I've grown in experience, and as you evolve into having more responsibilities you'll realise the difference between fixing your own mishaps and supporting other people with theirs.

I once attended a leadership course at the United States Defense University in Washington DC. One of my main insights from this was that when you're a leader and there's a crisis you should always 'head towards the sound of the guns'. In other words, be physically present so that you can witness and empathise with what's going on, because you'll make better decisions if you do. Usually it's not a leader's direct fault if something goes wrong, but it is their responsibility to be there to sort it out when it does. So often I see this not happening in the world, especially in politics. If you're the leader, be there in person.

In summary, we all make mistakes but it's what we do about them that matters. It's a lot easier for others to forgive them if you show you care about putting them right, and also learn from them so you don't go down the same path again.

WHAT WE COVERED

- Having a positive work ethic isn't the same as working hard (although it can be combined with it), it's about the level of engagement and commitment you give to your work.
- Someone with a positive work ethic excels in serving others, comes up with ideas, is involved with self-improvement, and is a helpful colleague.
- Working long hours is a problem if you feel burned out, but if you love your job and find it fulfilling you'll naturally want to be putting in the time.
- Make sure your manager is aware of your achievements.
- Mistakes will always happen, but it's the way you deal with them that matters.

AND JUST ASKING . . .

- What key aspect of your work ethic will you now choose to showcase?
- Can you pick an achievement that you'll make a point of highlighting at work as soon as possible?

CHAPTER 10

Ask for Help

Have you asked anyone for help today? If you're like most people, the answer is probably no. It's just something that we don't tend to do. This was brought home to me a few years ago when I shattered my ankle while climbing the Matterhorn, spending two months in a wheelchair and earning myself the nickname 'Wheelchairman'. I soon learned what it meant to be dependent on others for many of my basic needs, and how much I had always, in fact, relied on my family, friends and colleagues. Hopefully you won't need to go to this extreme to discover how valuable asking for help can be, because most work environments are the perfect places for people to help one another out.

It's strange how resistant we are to reaching out. Whenever I do it I find that people are usually more than willing to respond. If you have a career goal, want to learn something new, or have an ambition to start a fresh enterprise, there's always someone who can lend a hand. This means that there's a huge, untapped opportunity for you to advance and develop in your career, if only you're willing to put yourself out there.

There's no weakness in asking for help; in fact the oppo-site is true. It takes strength to admit that you can't do everything yourself. When you think about it, that's pretty obvious – why should you know how to do everything? I certainly don't. Even learning to ride a bike when you were a child meant someone holding the saddle, and most people are unsurprised when you need some assistance every now and then. Reaching out involves having the self-awareness to appreciate that you don't know it all, and the confidence to be open about it. Plus, it takes a little courage. All these qualities are attractive to other people and will put you in a positive light.

Often we worry that if we approach someone to ask for their time or expertise we'll be knocked back, but I bet if you think of any time when you've been asked by someone else, you were quite possibly flattered. Think about it: if a colleague asked you for a word of advice or half an hour of your day, and made it clear that it was because they thought you had something special to offer, would you tell them to go away? Of course not. I've always said that a team is a genius, and building a network of supporters is the perfect way to create your own.

THE BEAUTY OF ASKING FOR HELP

I remember the day when Martin Bean, then Vice-Chancellor of the Open University, paid me a visit. A warm, engaging man with a broad smile, he told me that he was wanting to develop an online learning initiative that would expand what the university could offer, giving free virtual lectures in partnership with other universities and institutions. His mission at that point was to ask as many people as he could in the training, development and employment space for input. 'What do you think about this idea?' he asked. 'And can you help?'

Because he was so open and charming, I had no hesitation in offering him my thoughts and ideas – in fact, I was flattered to be asked. As a result of this approach to information-gathering, Martin amassed a whole lot of feedback that was essential for his project. He also ended up establishing many new allies and contacts who were supportive of it, including me, because his call for help had created a bond between us. Eventually Martin and his team launched FutureLearn, a platform offering both free and paid-for courses on a vast array of subjects.

Martin showed some gall by asking for help, but he was able to do it because he didn't feel the need to give the impression that he already knew how to achieve his goal; he was secure enough to put himself out there and ask. All successful people do this. Senior business leaders realised long ago that from time to time it's a good idea to invite someone else into their organisation to ask them how they might improve, and this is why management consultancies are often successful. If the principle applies to the most substantial businesses in the world, it can certainly apply to us as individuals.

One of my favourite sources of advice is my entrepreneurs' group, which I've been meeting up with once a month for the past twenty years. The members all run businesses of their own, and we present ideas to one another and share our opportunities and challenges. I'll often ask for input when I'm not sure about the right direction for my company, or solicit suggestions about a personal or family issue I'm struggling with.

Long ago I sought the advice of the group when I wanted to take REED back into private ownership, but wasn't sure of the best way to do it or if it was right. The one thing I knew was that, if I went ahead with it, I and my team could re-create the unique family culture that had been a big part of the company's early success. We could also make bold decisions about how to spend our money, operating with a long-term view without the pressure of generating immedi-ate returns. Some members of my group had had personal experience of this situation, and their advice and support gave me the confidence to go ahead. I ended up bringing the company safely back into private hands, a decision that I've never regretted. One of my first decisions was to invest a seven-figure sum in a new digital recruitment service, something that would have been difficult to do with outside shareholders to account to.

Another benefit of asking for help is that, like the rest of us, you're coloured by your own experiences, and receiv-ing external input helps to balance them out. People who have no vested interest in your goals and ideas will be more objective – they'll point out flaws in your plans that you might never have spotted (perhaps because you didn't want to) and also bolster your confidence if they think you're on to a good thing. If you can find a similar group to mine that's relevant to you, it's helpful to build it into your life and work.

WHAT KIND OF HELP COULD YOU ASK FOR?

The nature of the help you could receive is unlimited, and that's what can make it difficult to know where to begin. Here are some ideas to kick-start your imagination, especially if you're not in the habit of asking.

If you're at the beginning of your career. You could approach an older and more experienced person who's successful in the field you're wanting to progress in. They can act as a mentor, helping you to navigate the unfamiliar world you've found yourself in. If they're a good one they'll also challenge you to make sure you're not settling for second best, and can act as a sounding board for any uncertainties that you have. It's easy to assume that older people don't have relevant ideas for your generation, but you'll find yourself the recipient of timeless wisdom and kind encouragement if you choose the right person. They might even introduce you to your next key contact.

If you're more experienced. There are lots of advantages in having ten or twenty years under your belt, but what happens when the next new app or software platform bursts on to the scene and you don't have a clue how to use it? This is when approaching a younger person can be a life-saver. They'll talk you through the pros and cons of what's on offer and help you understand it. They'll also be flattered that you, someone who they look up to as being more experienced, is willing to learn from them – it could be the start of a productive new relationship.

If you want help from a crowd of people. To gather material for three of my previous books, I asked for advice from hundreds of people and so have first-hand experience of the power of crowdsourcing. For instance, *The 7 Second CV*, my guide to writing a killer résumé, drew on feedback that I gained from countless recruiters on the best and worst CVs they'd ever seen. In a similar way, you can crowdfund your next project or charity venture by using the online tools available. I'm sure you've seen how generous people can be if they're convinced the cause is worthwhile. REED's charity website, The Big Give, has raised over £100 million through the power of crowdsourcing and matched funding.

If you're in a team. I haven't had a direct peer group in my business for a long time, and I'm quite envious of people who do. If you're struggling with your job, or feeling over-whelmed by a problem, why not ask the person sitting next to you for input? You can also absorb a lot of helpful infor-mation just by listening to what's going on around you. I've learned huge amounts from being around smart people who are doing interesting things and seeing how they approach problems or think about the issues of the day. Being alive to that kind of opportunity is a good thing.

If you have a personal problem. Because this kind of issue is so close to home it can sometimes feel overwhelming, so it's even more important to ask for help. Who could you trust to have your best interests at heart? It might be someone in your family, a trusted friend, or a neighbour – just give it a go and see what happens. You may be surprised.

THE BEST WAYS OF ASKING FOR HELP

When you don't know where to start it can be tempting to rush up to someone and say, 'I've got this terrible problem, can you help?' This is understandable, but try to see it from their point of view. It's best not to give them a loose end so they're fishing around for an answer. One of my friends, who's a management consultant, was recently approached by a colleague. 'I've had enough of this place,' the colleague said. 'But I don't know what on earth to do next.' My friend replied to him: 'Never, ever have a conversation like this until you've given it some thought first. Then ask for help.'

He was right. If the colleague had said instead, 'I'm interested in finding a new role in IT, or taking a different turn in my career. Do you know anyone who could help with this?' it would have given my friend something to go on. I'm often asked for career advice and if someone came to me saying, 'What kind of job should I apply for, James?' I can't really help. But if they said, 'I've decided I want a career in horse racing,' I'd put my mind to it and make some suggestions. You need to show that you've done some of the legwork yourself if you're to receive a helpful answer. The clearer your objective, the more positive the feedback will be.

Nothing trains you in this way of thinking more than management, as I've discovered when I've hired consultants for our business. I've been able to gain advice on areas as diverse as pricing, branding and monetising our digital assets, and it's all come down to knowing the right question to ask. In his book *Adventures of a Bystander*, management guru Peter Drucker recounts the story of Alfred Sloan, the legendary chairman of General Motors. He was chairing a meeting of GM's executive committee in which there was a debate about the suitability of a candidate to head up an operating division. It was a key role, and all agreed that the applicant in question had handled various crises superbly in his previous jobs – he seemed ideal for the post. Finally, Sloan interrupted. 'A very impressive record this man has,' he said. 'But do explain to me how he gets into all these crises he then so brilliantly surmounts?' While the committee was focusing on how the man had solved so many problems, Sloan was asking why he'd created them in the first place. Given that Sloan wanted someone to grow the company, not just to deal with problems, this was a critical distinction.

And finally, if at first you don't succeed with asking for help, try and try again. When you have a big ask it can take time to find someone who's willing to listen, so please don't feel discouraged if the response isn't positive from the off. If it's a yes that's great, and if not it doesn't matter because if you attempt it enough times, you'll eventually receive the answer you're looking for.

WHY IT'S HELPFUL TO BE HELPFUL

It goes without saying that the more helpful you are, the more likely people are to help you. This is because of the notion of reciprocity – it's part of our human nature. The theory is that if you do something for someone they're more likely to do the same for you one day, which is partly why people like giving favours. The more we give, the more we get. In his book *Yes! 50 Scientifically Proven Ways to be Persuasive* (co-authored with Noah Goldstein and Steve Martin), Robert Cialdini gives a powerful example of this. He recounts how social psychologist Dennis Regan carried out an experiment in which selected people received a surprise can of Coca-Cola from a stranger and were later asked to purchase some raffle tickets from the same person (with no reference to the gift). The ones who'd received the drink bought twice as many as those who hadn't.

This notion of reciprocity shows our bias towards fairness in our everyday interactions and relationships – it's part of the glue that holds our society together. Think about it – when you come to the end of your career, what will you remember most? How much money you earned, or all the people who gave you a hand along the way?

Unfortunately, some people have trouble with this, as I realised the other day when I witnessed an incident as surprising as it was depressing. Coming out of the London underground on a cold Monday morning, I was walking down the street towards my favourite coffee shop when I saw a homeless man sleeping in a doorway. He had a sleeping bag over him and was using a sheet of cardboard as a mattress. A plastic coffee cup was placed near his head for people to put money in. As I drew closer, I spotted a scrappy-looking man who went up to this cup as if he was going to give some money, but instead snatched what was in it for himself. Before he was challenged, the thief had hopped on to a bus. The homeless man had been asking for help in the most basic of ways, and was abused. I said to my assistant, who'd just moved to the capital from Lincolnshire, 'Welcome to London.'

Of course, there are altruistic reasons for helping people apart from what you'll receive in return. Professor and consultant Christine Porath has researched the impact of what she calls 'incivility' in the workplace, and has found that when people are treated with a lack of consideration, their performance reduces by 25 per cent and the number of ideas they come up with by 45 per cent. How you treat others is of importance, because your success is never just down to you as an individual.

The reality of life is that we help each other out all the time, even if we're not aware of it. The chair you're sitting on was made by people you'll never meet, the job you're doing is as a result of the earlier efforts of others, and the food you eat comes from the work of farmers and manufacturers around the world. When you think about it, the cycle of help is a wonderful thing and enables you to achieve your goals, whether it's having something to wear in the morning or finding the job of your dreams. Make the most of this by lending a hand to others too. As the saying goes, 'Be nice to people on the way up, because you'll meet them again on the way down.'

WHAT WE COVERED

- We don't tend to think about asking for help because we like to feel invincible.
- Often, the person we've asked is flattered and respects us for it.
- When you ask for help you can receive useful, objective advice that will help to balance out your own

biases and provide you with information for making decisions.

- Before you reach out to anyone, do a bit of ground-work first so that your request can be acted upon relatively easily.
- Being helpful is as important as asking for help – it's what makes the world go round.

AND JUST ASKING . . .

- When did you last ask for help?
- Is there something that you need help with now? Who could you approach to ask?

CHAPTER 11

Find a Boss You Can Learn From

Socrates taught Plato, Plato taught Aristotle, Aristotle taught Alexander the Great, and we're still talking about all four of them thousands of years later. In the same way, the smartest people know that despite their own knowledge, there are more experienced people who they can learn from to advance their careers. When was the last time you actively looked for a job opportunity that would lead to a rich learning experience, or even turned one down because it didn't offer one? If it's been a while, read on. Because framing the steps of your career as opportunities for learning brings rewards.

When you're starting out in your career, there's nothing more valuable than working for an inspirational boss or a knowledgeable expert because you have so much to learn from them. The saying 'Learn in your twenties, earn in your thirties' is valid for a reason. At first, it's more important to develop key skills and gain commercial awareness than it is to make pots of money. The more valuable experiences you're exposed to early on, the longer you will have to apply what you've learned, and the further in your career you'll travel in a short space of time.

Even if your twenties are behind you this is still relevant, because the more experienced you become the easier it can be to assume that you haven't so much to learn. This is a recipe for disaster. The world is changing so quickly that if you assume you know it all, you've more than likely had it – corporate history is littered with the failures of companies that didn't move with the times. It's not always straightforward to keep learning as you progress, but if you're in the frame of mind to develop yourself, you have a great chance of spotting any opportunities that come your way. These might take the form of working for someone you can learn a great deal from, or from immersing yourself in a situation which in itself is an expansive experience.

HOW I'VE LEARNED ON THE JOB

I'm lucky in that I grew up in an entrepreneurial family. Some of my earliest memories are of accompanying my father to his office during the school holidays or on the weekends (he always worked on Saturday mornings, opening his first business on Saturday, 7 May 1960). Soaking up the atmosphere and getting to know some of his first colleagues meant that I was beginning to learn how to succeed in business without even realising it. You might want to consider this when you think about how you can learn in your job. Who do you share your day with? It might be a colleague who works in an admirable way, or interacts with people with ease. One of the most interesting opportunities is to see how they approach the challenges and opportunities that come their way – what can you take from that?

My father is a high-energy individual who puts much emphasis on having ideas and on going out and meeting people to ask questions and gain input. I've picked up on that over the years I've spent with him, and now I run the business myself I often drop in on our offices unannounced because I want to know what it's like for our customers who will do the same. From these visits I gain three things: information (by finding out what's going on), ideas (by listening to the suggestions people make), and inspiration (by hearing motivational stories about what they've accomplished). It's essential that I stay informed, creative and driven.

Another job from which I learned a lot in my early career was as a media planner and buyer for the advertising agency Saatchi & Saatchi, which was at the time the most successful in the world. My role was to buy the media space for the adverts that the copywriters and designers had created, which involved talking to TV stations, magazines, newspapers and radio broadcasters.

In the process I learned a huge amount about negotiation. For a start, I discovered that the quality of the outcome for any deal depended largely on what questions I asked, or even on whether I asked any questions at all. For instance, if I checked whether we could gain a discount for booking a run of adverts, or whether they had any last-minute cancellations, I would be offered a good price. I also discovered that if I wasn't prepared to walk away from a deal, my negotiating power was wiped out. There was also the human element, as it became apparent to me that I could gain a better offer if the seller liked me just because I was friendly or had made them laugh, and this taught me about the power of relationships in business.

Even now, when a colleague says that they've negotiated the best deal they can, I normally tell them to go back and try again because it almost certainly isn't the case. I always encourage people to ask for more, even if they think they've taken it as far as they can.

THE BODY SHOP

One of my richest learning experiences, however, was working for Anita Roddick and her husband Gordon not long after they launched The Body Shop, an exciting new venture which sold affordable and natural cosmetics. I'd just graduated from college when I read an article about Anita winning Business Woman of the Year. This intrigued me. I did my homework on the business and learned more about its ethical credentials, which were centred on no animal testing for its products and on trading fairly with suppliers in the developing world. This distinctive position-ing was rapidly winning the The Body Shop customers, and it appealed me to because it was based on an eye-catching, game-changing story. I was becoming aware of the power of fast-flowing water in business, so I could see that the company represented a huge learning experience for me and would be an exciting place to work.

I was hopeful that the Roddicks would need help with their growing venture, and, not wanting to compete with other applicants who would no doubt apply for jobs that they advertised, I decided to be proactive. In those days, job applications were paper based, so I printed out my CV and posted it with a covering letter, saying that I would love to work for an entrepreneur and learn how to be one myself one day.

I was at home the following Saturday morning when Anita herself phoned and asked me, 'Can you come in for an interview on Monday?' My answer was an emphatic 'Yes.' At my interview she asked me a few questions and then said, 'We need someone to look after various projects here. When can you start?' I began the next day.

It was inspiring to be around such a dynamic couple who managed to combine both expansive energy and attention to detail. This was underpinned by Anita's approach to business. She was filled with ideas and cared passionately about what she did and the way she did it. Her husband Gordon was a great partner for her as he brought complementary management skills to the company, and together they made an invincible team.

My work was based on managing projects to help take The Body Shop forward. One of them was evaluating their franchise strategy – should they expand it, and what were the pros and cons? This involved me travelling to meet their franchisees, which took me to parts of the United Kingdom that I'd never seen before. This included my first visit to Scotland. I also worked in the shops as an assistant, so I gained experience from the ground up. It was sobering to see the commitment that went into the cashing up at the end of each day, for instance. If the takings in the till drawer and the amount entered into the till didn't reconcile, I had to do it again and again until they did, or there had to be a watertight explanation for it. I respected that.

Now that I run a company with offices from Aberdeen to Plymouth, I can see that I've learned a lot of useful ways of working from my time at The Body Shop. Some people complain about business leaders living in ivory towers, but my training from both my father and the Roddicks has made sure that I keep my feet firmly on the shop floor. I also learned about positioning a business in a unique and creative way so that it stands out, and running it consistently with that ethos. Looking back, the Roddicks were thirty years ahead of their time in creating a brand with a driving purpose, and I was very lucky to have been a small part of that.

Ask yourself, 'What can I learn from those around me, both in my workplace and beyond?' Everyone will have something to give, so don't let up until you have found out what it is.

WHY YOU SHOULD BE PAID TO LEARN

Despite benefiting from an education at Oxford University and Harvard Business School, I do believe that I've learned more from the handful of inspiring people I've worked closely with over the years than I have from either of those great institutions. No course can really teach you how to deal with people – how to engage with them, gain the best from them, encourage them and enthuse them. Creating a shared purpose for what you do is fundamental to success in any walk of life and we all have to find ways of learning about that, whether we end up running a football team, a company or a cottage hospital. Even if all you're in charge of is the stationery cupboard, it's essential to understand its purpose.

By the end of your career you'll have spent considerably more years working than studying. The irony is that it takes time and money to go to college or university, but if you find brilliant people to work with and for, you can learn so much more on the job. Effectively, you're being paid to learn. Think about what you can absorb from a job that you could never pick up at school or college:

- knowledge about your industry,
- how to delight clients and customers,
- strategic thinking,
- giving presentations,
- public speaking,
- how to get on with and manage a wide variety of people, and
- how to organise your time and set priorities.

I'm not against the idea of higher education – far from it – but I've always found it interesting to see how some people who work for me manage to do extremely well without it. One of my senior managers started off at a retailer, earning £7 an hour as a temporary sales assistant. She was asked to become permanent because she was so good at her job, so she asked her father for advice. Should she do that or go to university? He said, 'Say you'll join them permanently only if they put you on a graduate-level package.' Which they duly did. So she rose straight from earning £7 an hour to £28,000 a year without the intervening years at university. After the retailer she worked for an inspiring manager at a tech firm, learned a huge amount from him and is now, at the age of twenty-nine, filling a valuable role for us on a six-figure salary. If she'd taken the conventional route she'd have studied an academic subject at a Russell Group university, graduated, looked for a job, and doubtless obtained one on a graduate training scheme. Which would have been fine, but there's little chance that she'd be where she is now at her age.

FINDING SOMEONE TO LEARN FROM

Wherever you work, try to put yourself into situations in which there are people who have a reputation for great leadership, motivation, or both. Breathe the same air and you can't help but absorb information from them. There are various ways of doing this.

When you apply for a job, one of your key criteria should be what you're going to learn from it. This can take the form of the person or people you'll be working with, or the nature of the work itself. In my experience, not enough people think like this. If you want to be an accountant, for instance, consider not only which firm you'd like to work for, but also who in that firm you would want as your boss. There's nothing more exciting than working for someone who you can learn a lot from. I loved my time with the Roddicks because I knew I wanted to be inspired by entrepreneurs, and that was something I couldn't find at school. But if your thing is brain surgery, working with a top brain surgeon is probably a good idea. If you've done your research you'll not only be more likely to work somewhere fulfilling, but also to impress your interviewers with your knowledge about the role.

Then, when you go for an interview, ask yourself if the person in the opposite chair is someone you could be impressed by. If the answer is 'no', you should seriously consider whether you want to take the job. If all you'll receive from the role is money or a fancy title, think again. What could you put into the place and what could it put into you? You can spend your pay cheque in one weekend, but when you learn something new you have it for the rest of your life.

If you're already in a job, you can stand out by being clear about what you want. Again, not enough people do this and it's always impressive when someone says they have a hunger to learn and succeed. Tell your manager that your goal is to develop in a specific way or to be promoted – whatever will help you move forward. They can then help you to achieve it. When I think of the people who work with us, I realise that I have no way of knowing what their hopes and dreams are unless I ask them and they choose to tell me. If someone says that they want to develop a new skill and asks if there's a way of working this out together, I'm happy to talk to them about it because I usually find that their interests are aligned with ours. It can suit an organisation as much as an individual when people want to progress.

What should you do if you're stuck in a dead-end job in which you're not learning anything new? Find another one, because you have to take charge of your own learning. Or seek a promotion in the place you work right now, even if it's only a small step up. If this feels a bit extreme, there are alternative options. If you're under-stretched, you could ask for more responsibility or to go on a training course – even one that you do in your own time. Is there someone who could mentor you, or whom you could shadow to learn from for a while? If you approach them the answer may be yes (and if not now, possibly in the future). You're on their radar.

This goes both ways. If you're in a position to help someone else to learn, consider offering your experience. After all, learning is a cumulative, social process. Each generation of leaders and experts doesn't start off that way, they get there by developing themselves. I was once invited to talk on BBC Radio as our company had started a scheme to help long-term unemployed people into work. The presenter challenged me by saying that it was a waste of time because there were no jobs for them in any case. Interestingly, we'd only been open a week or two but we'd already unearthed a thousand vacancies in the area, and we'd achieved this by asking local employers a simple question. 'If you think back on your career, someone once gave you your first opportunity. Will you consider doing the same for someone else?' It was the Roddicks who were kind enough to give me a job all that time ago.

Finally, it's worth keeping track of what you've learned. Richard Branson famously carries a notebook to jot down his ideas and discoveries – in fact, one of his greatest regrets when his Necker Island home burned down was that he lost them all in the fire. But even if you never look at your notes again (and I hope you do), there's something about writing things down that embeds them in your head more effectively than just thinking about them. They become ingrained in your mind, influencing your daily actions and potentially guiding the trajectory of your whole career.

WHAT WE COVERED

- Whether you're at the beginning or middle of your career, continuous learning and development are critical to your success and fulfilment.
- Every job gives you opportunities to learn.
- Although education is worthwhile, it can't teach you everything you need to know in the world of work.
- Learning through doing means that you're being paid to learn in your job.
- When you apply for a role, consider first what you're going to learn from it.

AND JUST ASKING . . .

- Who gave you your first work opportunity, and could you do the same for someone else?
- Is there someone you could learn a great deal from, and whom you could offer to help in exchange for what you would gain?

CHAPTER 12

Change Your Job and Change Your Life

This is where we come full circle. Your job dictates where you spend your waking hours, who you spend them with, and what you spend them doing. It either energises and fulfils you, or it turns you into a grouch who comes home each day in a grumpy mood. At REED our purpose is 'Improving Lives Through Work', and our brand message is 'Love Mondays', because we believe that there's a great job out there for everyone – it's just a matter of finding it.

Sadly, plenty of people don't love Mondays and this is something that bothers me. Waking every day to the prospect of nothing but boredom or frustration ahead of you – I can't imagine anything worse. So change it. We've all been there, and I don't think there's anyone who's been blissfully happy throughout their career. My father told me that he was a failure until the age of twenty-three. What changed? He started a new job, and if you're not happy in yours, you should too. It might be that there's someone in your organisation who's making your life a misery, or maybe you just need a new scene. Whatever it is, don't push it aside and hope for the best – do something about it.

Enjoying what you do for a living is also fundamental to your career success, because you're more likely to do well if you feel a spring in your step as you go into work. The energy you put into it will be returned to you by your organisation. You'll also be a more supportive friend and partner to those you share your life with, because there will be reserves left in the tank at the end of each day to give to them. This means that changing jobs can be transformational.

MAKE THE CHANGE

Because you change everything when you change your job, I'm always surprised when I see people putting less effort into researching their next career move than they do into choosing a holiday or buying a new television. Your work time is everything, and how you spend it will be important to you.

Your first step is to become clear on why you want a new job in the first place. What's wrong with your current situation? Is it the nature of your work that's getting you down, the boss you report to, your colleagues, the organisational culture or are you just frustrated and in need of a fresh challenge? Maybe you're not unhappy as such, but feel the need to progress your career before you become so (in which case, congratulations for being proactive).

It's helpful to understand this first, because it will have an influence on what you do next. If you like your workplace but could do with a different type of role, then an internal move might be an option, but if you're wanting to shift into a different sector or escape from a boss who's driving you mad, you'll need to look elsewhere. If it's a pay rise you're after, you may find that moving companies is your only choice. Wages have been static for so long that it can be hard to achieve a significant rise by negotiating with your manager or by staying in the same organisation. Many companies, however, are willing to offer a premium to attract fresh talent.

In short, there are countless motivations for moving jobs, but whatever yours is, it's a key life decision. A pivotal moment. We only live once and we only have one working life, so it's important that it's a positive one. What's more, there's a job out there for everyone – no one is unemployable. Some people may say that's naive, but in my twenty-five years of working in recruitment I can honestly say that's been my experience.

In fact, our company has been making a specific effort to help long-term unemployed people into work for twenty-two years now. I remember one man, Anthony, who gained a job as a security guard through us after being out of work for fifteen years. He bravely volunteered to speak at a large conference that the government was organising, during which he recounted how demoralising it had been to be unemployed for so long. He also said that the new job in the security firm had changed his life, and that for the first time in years he'd been able to buy his children Christmas presents. Needless to say there wasn't a dry eye in the house, and he received a standing ovation.

I also met another man, Dave, a serial offender who'd

spent twenty years of his adult life in jail for various offences including armed robbery. He had joined one of our programmes after his release from prison, and gained a job working on the railways as part of the night maintenance crew. When I asked him how he found working nights, he looked at me as if I was daft. 'I've always worked nights!' he replied. More seriously, he told me that he'd been within hours of accepting a job as a getaway driver for a criminal associate, and that if he hadn't started work on the railways he'd probably have accepted it. 'This has changed my life,' he said. 'Because now, when there's a knock on the door, I'm not worrying if it's the police coming to take me back to prison.'

These stories are dramatic, and I expect (and hope) that your situation is less so. But whether you're unemployed or already in a job, your focus should be on working out what you want and then going for it. As an example, today on reed.co.uk there are more than 250,000 new job vacancies, so there could well be one that suits you. Your next step is to look around and see what's out there, whether it be advertised roles or using your network to dig out opportunities. At this point it pays to be flexible in your outlook, because the ideal role that you have in mind may not be available right now. That's OK. Ambitions have a habit of coming to fruition if you keep them alive for long enough – your next job might be a stepping stone to the real deal.

It's also worth considering moving geographical area if you need to. This is something that many people are reluctant to do, maybe because of the costs involved or the concern about uprooting their lives. But especially if you're in your twenties and don't have a family of your own, it can be life-changing. One of my best friends moved to America when he was thirty and has now married and had a family out there. His career has benefitted hugely, and it was all because he wasn't afraid to make that transition. Nor does it have to be a permanent shift. My last assistant moved to London from Middlesbrough via Yorkshire, and it wouldn't surprise me if she later ends up back in the north-east where her family lives. If she does, she'll have gained valuable experience in London in the meantime.

Although changing organisations is a great way to progress, so is staying put. Imagine this scenario: you join an accountancy firm as a trainee and end up being promoted to partner many years later. What does that say about your personal equity within that organisation? It shows that you've been a great problem-solver and asset over the years, and no doubt have an excellent reputation as well. If you love where you are but have ambitions to do more, you could do worse than build your personal brand as a knowledgeable and proactive person at your existing company.

HOW TO LEAVE

Resigning from a job sounds simple – all you have to do is tell your boss, hand over the fateful letter, and that's it, right? From a practical point of view that's correct, but there's a bit more to it if you're thinking about your career long term.

When you depart an organisation you leave behind a 'you' shaped hole where you used to be. This hole then starts to be filled by your colleagues' memories and impressions of you. How will they talk about you when you're gone? What impression will you leave behind? This is important because you want to carry a good reputation with you to your new job. The last thing you need is to arrive at your next workplace to find people's attitudes towards you slowly shifting as negative rumours from your previous company filter through.

If you're leaving because you don't like your boss, that's understandable, but try not to make an issue of it. Similarly with your colleagues. The world isn't a big place and people talk to one another, so if you walk out of a company on bad terms this can come back to bite you. Unfortunately, you're the one who will end up being harmed. On the other hand, if you leave on good terms, saying to your manager, 'I've had a great career here but now I want to move on,' they'll almost certainly respect that.

The way in which you leave should be a continuation of the way you do your job – carried out with respect, integrity and professionalism. If you were a business, you'd have a balance sheet with assets and liabilities recorded, and the individual equivalent of that is your personal equity – the sum of who you are. The more you have on the positive side (the ideas you've come up with, the contributions of substance that you've made, the help you've given) the more solid your reputation will be. This makes you more valuable than someone who has coasted over the years and done the minimum.

Some people even return to their previous organisation after they've left – this has certainly happened at our company. It might be because a new opportunity opens up which they want to take advantage of, or the person they were escaping from makes their own external move. From your point of view, it's worth knowing that companies tend to keep records of previous staff so it's important that yours are positive. Also, new employers often ask for references of previous bosses with the question 'would you rehire this person?' If you were to leave your present role and then return, do you think you'd be welcomed back with open arms? It's a telling question.

Your relationships with your colleagues are another aspect of your equity that you can take with you to a new job. These people might be helpful to you in many ways – as supporters, advisers, customers or simply as reputation-enhancers. To say nothing of how much easier it would be to return (or even to bump into them in the street) if you've left on friendly terms. It's impressive when someone has maintained good relationships throughout their career.

All this might seem obvious to you, but I often come across people for whom it's not. So often, individuals make the mistake of not leaving well. Not long ago someone who worked for our company left to start their own recruitment agency. That was fine and I wished them well, but when I discovered that they had stolen our data to give themselves a head start, we were compelled to take legal action against them. This resulted in them having to close their new business. It was so unnecessary. Now they can't find a job anywhere in the recruitment world, because their reputation has travelled with them. You can't leave somewhere in a mess and expect it not to follow you around.

Leaving well is such an important thing, and can be easily forgotten in the heady excitement of moving to a new job. Thanking your boss and colleagues for all they've given you, and avoiding ruffling any feathers unnecessarily, really does pay off. Just think, if one of your existing team members were to re-emerge in your new organisation in two years' time, you'd be glad you'd taken the trouble.

THE HIDDEN ADVANTAGES OF GOING TEMPORARY

Some time ago we carried out research for the Chartered Institute of Personnel and Development, presenting our findings at their annual conference. The subject was whether temporary workers are as happy as permanent ones, or less so. We surveyed individuals in both areas and, interestingly, the people doing temporary work were happier than those in permanent roles. I think that might have been because the temporaries had more control and flexibility around how they spent their time. If you're temporary and decide you would like a week off or not to work next Thursday, that's your decision. You can take a raincheck. In a permanent job you have to ask your boss for permission and make sure you're fitting in with your team. When we gave our talk on the topic lots of people were surprised, even suspicious, of the findings (after all, we do own a temporary agency). A few of them then went off and did their own research, but tellingly they came back with the same conclusion.

I tell you this because I often come across the view that temporary jobs are insecure or unfulfilling, and therefore best avoided. It's true that you don't have the long-term commitment from your organisation that you do with permanent work, but a 'long-term' job can end at any point. In reality, no job is permanent. If your agency knows that you're a good worker they'll definitely keep you busy, but if you're made redundant from a permanent role you're on your own.

Pretty much all fields have temporary workers in them: administration, commercial driving, health and medicine, retail, teaching, technology – you name it. We've even supplied temporary detectives to the police force from a pool of retired officers who want to work the hours they like. This might be worth considering if you're coming to the end of your career and wanting to downshift from full to part time. You could move into a series of short-term roles that allow you to flex your hours.

So much work stress is caused by not being in control of your situation. If you feel trapped in your permanent job but are wary (rightly) of jumping into the first full-time opportunity that comes your way, temping is an excellent option. You'll build up experience working in different environments, thereby learning what you like and don't like, and training yourself to be flexible at the same time. You might even be hired permanently by the company you're in if they like you enough, and, importantly, if you like them too.

I hope this helps you to feel less fearful about the prospect of moving out and moving on, because there are a number of routes that you can take. No job is for ever, temporary or permanent, so the more visibility you have of your options the better.

A JOB, A BETTER JOB, A CAREER

I once read a brilliant book called *No One is Unemployable* by Debra Angel, about helping long-term unemployed people back into work. Her approach was what she called 'work first'. She realised that the reason many people weren't in work wasn't because they didn't have skills; it was because their mindset wasn't in the right place. They'd become demotivated and this led to them becoming excluded from the labour market. Her catchphrase, which I love, is: 'A job, a better job, a career.' This can apply to anyone, unemployed or not. First you make a start, then you make progress by being promoted or moving to a better job, and before you know it you have a career.

Central to progressing your life's work is recognising that a job is a problem to be solved, but a career is when you become a problem solver in a particular area. What does this mean? Well, the reason anyone is offered a job is simply because someone needs help. It might be practical (those boxes won't pack themselves) or intellectual (that IT software won't debug itself), but either way it's a challenge looking for a resolution. When you show yourself to be proficient in solving that problem, you can move on to the next one and the next one after that. Once you've solved a string of problems that have something in common with each other, such as a specialist expertise or a particular ability, you build a CV that proves you're an asset to your boss and team-mates.

The pressure on all of us is to come up with ideas and innovations for solving these difficult questions posed by our work, and those people who develop the ability to do that and who have an appetite for it will find themselves doing well because there aren't that many of them. They're the ones who will percolate to the top of all sorts of organisations, and they'll do so partly because they don't think they know it all. They have a growth mindset.

Everyone deserves to have a career that makes them happy, but it won't come about through wishing. We're all sometimes guilty of coming up with brilliant plans and not following them through to the finish, so don't let this be you. Nor should you feel under pressure to achieve it all right now – it's called a job, a better job, a career for a reason. If you take on board the inspiration and advice in this book, put it into practice, and use it to gain your next fulfilling role, you'll be taking charge of your career before you know it.

You may also find it helpful to read *The 7 Second CV: How to Land the Interview*, my book about how to write the CV that puts you in the interview chair, and *Why You? 101 Interview Questions You'll Never Fear Again*, which gives you the inside track on how to succeed at interview. Both will be an asset to you as you focus on securing your dream job.

For now is the time to embark on the journey of your career. Do your best to enjoy it, and one day remember to look back on all you've experienced and accomplished along the way. What will you see? Your life's work.

WHAT WE COVERED

- Enjoying your work is key to your happiness in life.
- If you don't love what you do, you must move on.
- When you resign from a role, do so with professionalism

and good grace so that your good reputation travels with you.

- Temporary work can be an excellent short- or long-term option.
- A job is a problem to be solved, so if you become good at solving a particular kind of problem you have the basis of a successful career.

AND JUST ASKING . . .

- Would you consider temporary work as opposed to a permanent role?
- If you're thinking of leaving your job, do you think your manager would rehire you in the future?

THE 60 GOLDEN CAREER NUGGETS

At the beginning of this book I promised you sixty invaluable tips to help you to forge a successful career. You'll find five of them at the end of each chapter, but I'm summarising them here so they're all in one place. They're insights that I've learned on the road of life rather than from formal education, and my hope is that they will power you on your own career journey too. When you're feeling a little lost or your tank is running low, why not dip into them and see if they re-charge your purpose? Enjoy the ride.

LOOK IN THE MIRROR

- Self-reflection is the vital first step in planning your career, because it's only through self-knowledge that you'll be able to make the right decisions.

- First, look in a physical mirror and learn to appreciate yourself.

- Second, identify your loves and hates, which provide the power source for your progress.

- Third, work out your values, which give you fulfilment in your work.

- Fourth, pinpoint your purpose, which will steer you in the right direction.

GO TO PARTIES

- You never know when you're about to meet the person who might change your life, so it's important to put yourself in front of as many people as possible.

- Going to parties gives you opportunities to enrich your life and career.

- There are many ways to discover parties to attend, such as following your interests, searching online, using your professional networks, and volunteering.

- Even if you don't feel like going, just do it.

- There are lots of ways to start conversations at parties, and it's easier if you're prepared with a few lines.

PLAY POOHSTICKS

- When you locate your career in fast-growing industries or sectors, you'll be more likely to progress quickly, and with less effort, than if you choose a declining industry.

- The same goes for job roles that are in growth, even if they're in mature sectors.

- You can always find a way of matching your talents and

skills to fast-flowing industries, even if it's not the most obvious option.

- Finding sectors and job roles that are in the early stages of growth isn't easy; if it were, everyone would be doing it. Keep your eyes and ears open and talk to people.

- Certain areas will always be in demand, even if they're not in growth.

BE SELFISH

- Being sustainably selfish means doing work you enjoy so that both you and your organisation benefit.

- When you're not sustainably selfish in your job, you're likely to burn out.

- Although money is important it's rarely the main reason most people do a job – you have to enjoy it too.

- There are nine feel-good fundamentals for sustainable work: doing what you enjoy, having good colleagues, having the opportunity to try new things, being able to make a difference, doing work with meaning, having fun, working close to home, being yourself and finding a well-fitting culture.

- You can build a sustainably selfish career by cultivating self-awareness, talking to people about opportunities at great workplaces, looking after yourself physically, and managing your time and responses in a healthy way.

KICK-START SOME GOOD HABITS AND KICK OUT SOME BAD ONES

- Habits are powerful because they dictate what we think and do, day after day.

- Your good habits give you energy and positivity, whereas your bad ones sap your strength and remove opportunities from your path.

- Some good habits are being cheerful, carrying out regular self-reviews, rising early, keeping healthy, avoiding procrastination, being open-minded, and being grateful.

- Some bad habits are being a complainer, becoming an addict, and not taking enough exercise.

- Changing a habit is a three-step process: identify the ones you want to change, work out what rewards you gain from them, and replace them with ones you would like to have instead.

PICK YOUR TARGETS

- Goals shape your life, so it's worth making sure that you have positive ones.

- When you set yourself a target, make it a challenging one and you'll achieve more than you think.

- To choose your targets, start with your values, passions and purpose.

- Then visualise where you want to end up and work out the steps to travelling there.

- Once you've achieved what you want, start the next journey!

THINK IN DAYS AND DECADES

- Being focused on the day today, and also on what you want to achieve in ten years' time, is the key to being the successful creator of your career.

- From eighteen to thirty your focus is on trying different things, travelling and learning.

- From thirty to fifty your focus is on making the most of your experience and moving yourself up to the next level.

- From fifty to seventy your focus is on planning your legacy and using this last opportunity to fulfil your potential.

- It's just as important to live in the present moment as it is to plan for the years ahead.

BE POWERFUL, BE PREPARED

- Being prepared gives you power because you can take advantage of positive situations and make the best of negative ones.

- The most common situations in which it's important to be well prepared are job interviews, presentations and meetings of various kinds.

- When you have a job interview, take the time to research the organisation and think about the answers you would give to questions beforehand.

- When you make a presentation, rehearsing your message is essential for winning over your audience.

- When you're being introduced to someone for the first time, or in an important meeting, knowing your objectives and something about the other person enables you to come across as knowledgeable and credible.

SHOWCASE YOUR WORK ETHIC

- Having a positive work ethic isn't the same as working hard (although it can be combined with it), it's about the level of engagement and commitment you give to your work.
- Someone with a positive work ethic excels in serving others, comes up with ideas, is involved with self-improvement, and is a helpful colleague.
- Working long hours is a problem if you feel burned out, but if you love your job and find it fulfilling you'll naturally want to be putting in the time.
- Make sure your manager is aware of your achievements.
- Mistakes will always happen, but it's the way you deal with them that matters.

ASK FOR HELP

- We don't tend to think about asking for help because we like to feel invincible.

- Often, the person we've asked is flattered and respects us for it.

- When you ask for help you can receive useful, objective advice that will help to balance out your own biases and provide you with information for making decisions.

- Before you reach out to anyone, do a bit of ground-work first so that your request can be acted upon relatively easily.

- Being helpful is as important as asking for help – it's what makes the world go round.

FIND A BOSS YOU CAN LEARN FROM

- Whether you're at the beginning or middle of your career, continuous learning and development are critical to your success and fulfilment.

- Every job gives you opportunities to learn.

- Although education is worthwhile, it can't teach you everything you need to know in the world of work.

- Learning through doing means that you're being paid to learn in your job.

- When you apply for a role, consider first what you're going to learn from it.

CHANGE YOUR JOB AND CHANGE YOUR LIFE

- Enjoying your work is key to your happiness in life.

- If you don't love what you do, you must move on.

- When you resign from a role, do so with professionalism and good grace so that your good reputation travels with you.

- Temporary work can be an excellent short- or long-term option.

- A job is a problem to be solved, so if you become good at solving a particular kind of problem you have the basis of a successful career.

ACKNOWLEDGEMENTS

The origins of the book *Life's Work* are from a talk entitled 'How to get your career off to a flying start' that I've been giving to groups of students and young people for a number of years now. These ideas have developed over time to the extent that I can now confidently describe them as '12 Proven Ways to Fast Track Your Career'. Why? Because in my experience they definitely work. *Life's Work* is, therefore, the result of countless questions, conversations and observations from more than half a century of living and working. I would like to acknowledge it as such and to thank all the people who have participated in the journey so far.

In particular, I would like to thank my colleagues at REED who are my extended family and from whom I learn new things every day. I would also like to thank my publishers Little, Brown and especially my editor Tom Asker whose enthusiasm for this project and whose ideas and suggestions have encouraged me to keep working on this manuscript right up to the very last deadline. I would like to thank the team who worked so closely with me to put these ideas down on paper, especially Ginny Carter, Laura Holden, Molly Mitchell and Imogen Burgess. And, of course, my agent Robert Smith whose thoughtful insights are always encouraging and helpful.

Thank you to the first readers and reviewers of the manuscript, Melanie Martin, Caroline Slatten Larsson and Jeff Scott. You made it better. Thank you to Mladen Petreski for your thoughts on why we find ourselves where we are and to Nina Bhatia, Heather Melville and Anita Mortimer for sharing your own career journeys and the lessons you learned.

In my early career I was lucky enough to have some very inspirational and patient bosses from whom I learned a lot. I would particularly like to thank Anita and Gordon Roddick at The Body Shop; Jenny Soph and Peter Setterington at Saatchi & Saatchi; Juliet Vergos and Jackie Wray at Afghanaid; and Brian Davies and David Dawson at the BBC. Not all of these people are still living, but they all made an indelible mark on me.

The Young Presidents Organisation has helped me for more than the twenty years I have been a member. I would like to thank my entrepreneurs' forum and, in particular, John Ayton, Neville Brauer, Jonathan Mills, Will Ramsay, David Roche and Martin Scott for all the support you continue to give me.

I would also like to thank Michael Green and Paul Stoltz for being such brilliant business coaches at times in my career when I was struggling to find answers. You helped me to ask different questions and to be more creative in my thinking. I would like to thank David Fitzsimons for your consistent friendship, advice and support. You helped me to find my voice. And thank you to Paul Weiland for your friendship and marketing genius. 'Love Mondays' would not have been born and bounced into life without you.

Health and fitness are important to me. Thank you

Dr Alix Daniel and Dr Ingrid Eysn for your enlightened approach to preventative medicine and thank you to top trainers, Stefi Cossetti and Nadia Staley for all those early morning sessions in the gym. I wouldn't have done them without you.

Lastly and most importantly, I would like to thank my family. My mother Adrianne Reed and father Alec Reed, for teaching me so much and making so many things possible. Thank you. My wife Nicola, always so creative and encouraging, you are my enduring inspiration. Thank you. And our children who are so quick to make suggestions and never too shy to point out ways that I might improve. Thank you. I am full of love and admiration for you all.

INDEX